Endorsements

In *What's God Really Like?*, S. J. Hill invites us to become fascinated by God and, in that fascination, to move beyond the fear-based themes that have so often distorted our image of God. With a focus on Jesus and Scripture, Hill paints a portrait of a God who is "holy wild" and overflowing with generous love and contagious joy. This book is a welcome and timely remedy to the unworthy portraits of God that have too often haunted our imaginations.

Brian Zahnd
Lead pastor of Word of Life Church in St. Joseph, MO
and author of *Sinners in the Hands of a Loving God*

What if God—the *actual* God—can laugh and dance? What if the One True God is affectionate rather than angry, beautiful rather than ugly, deliberately weak instead of a cosmic bully? Good news: S. J. Hill knows this God and is willing to introduce us to Him in his book, *What's God Really Like?* S. J. walks us into an accessible experience of the Abba who is intimate and playful. Relational theology at its finest.

Brad Jersak, PhD
Author of *A More Christlike God*

S. J. Hill has given us a God-burst of love and joy in his newest release, *What's God Really Like?* Wait until you read this powerful book! It will bring God's smile into your heart. Engaging, potent, captivating—these are all words I could use to describe my experience in reading this manuscript. Wow! The lid just blew off my mind as I read each chapter full of insights into God's heart of love for each of us. This book needs to be read by everyone as it uncovers such beautiful truth about the God we love. Leave religion at the door and cross over into finding out for yourself *What God is Really Like*! It will change you.

Dr. Brian Simmons
Passion & Fire Ministries; The Passion Translation Project

Many years ago when I was a student in Bible College, I heard S. J. Hill speak and was deeply impacted and challenged by his teaching. I had heard many preachers over the years—but never someone like him. Few men embody a "word from the Lord" the way S. J. does. Over the years his focus on God's love and affections for humanity has not changed but has only grown stronger and sharper than ever. His new offering, *What's God Really Like?*, is the clearest representation yet of a God that many Christians have never known. It's the kind of book that has the potential to change your life, and it contains a message that can change the world.

Daniel Kolenda
President and CEO of Christ for all Nations

For literally centuries, the gospel in western Christianity (especially Reformation Protestantism) has been presented to the world through the lenses of legal, criminal, and courtroom concepts. The result has embedded an incomplete, inaccurate, imbalanced, unduly severe, and unattractive image of God into popular consciousness. A robust theology of beauty is, and has been, conspicuously absent in much western theology. S. J. Hill has wonderfully addressed this shortcoming in *What's God Really Like?* I am so thankful for people like S. J. who are reawakening western believers to the beauty of the Lord Jesus and His invitation to enjoy His life with and in the Father.

Stephen R. Crosby, D. Min.
Author, www.stevecrosby.org; www.stevecrosby.com

One of life's age-old questions is, "If there is a God, what's He like?" In S. J. Hill's new book, *What's God Really Like?*, he pulls back one veil after another, allowing us to see a God that few authors have ever described. This God actually laughs and is joyful beyond anything we've ever seen. He even dances. I love it! Even more, I love this book! One of my favorite quotes from this wonderfully animated book is simply this, "Jesus changed the way men perceived God...so we might know Him as He really is and no longer be victims of our own misunderstandings." Thank you S. J. for helping us see Him as He truly is!

Chris DuPré
Pastor, songwriter, and author of *The Wild Love of God*

S. J. Hill has unveiled a revolutionary reality so many have missed or forgotten. God is happy. Since I was a child and first heard the story of the prodigal son, I saw one simple point. The Father just wanted to dance with His son. As I've spent a lifetime hearing messages on the prodigal, few seemed to care about what the Father ultimately wanted. The focus was always on the hog pen, on the speech of repentance, the restored robe and ring, and of course the bitter elder brother. As viable as each of these points is, the point of the dancing, joyful, happy Father is rarely prioritized. Imagine my delight when I read from the heart of a writer who has clearly had an encounter with the joyful Father. I believe this book will usher you out of the hog pen of your own striving, and out of the backyard of your own bitterness, and into the healing arms of a Father who just wants to dance with His sons and daughters.

Bill Vanderbush
Pastor, Community Presbyterian Church, Celebration, FL, author and speaker

In the beginning, God created man in His image, and man returned the favor. Down through the ages, His image has been tampered with by artists, politicians, and theologians. We have ended up with a not so attractive or enticing God. Nietzche said that he would only believe in a God who knows how to dance. I'm pretty sure that Nietzche would like the image of God presented in S. J. Hill's latest book, *What's God Really Like?* Refuting the prevalent view of an angry God, S. J. unveils the true God, as revealed to us through His Son. S. J. takes our breath away with poetic images of a dancing, laughing God who enjoys being in the presence of His people.

For those of you who find yourself entangled in a web of shame and guilt, you will quickly be drawn toward the Father portrayed in this book, a loving Father waiting to pull you into His wondrous embrace where you will feel the kiss of divine compassion. Thank you, S. J., for the time and effort you put into writing this book, answering our questions, and filling our hearts with Father's love.

Don Milam
Acquisitions Consultant, Whitaker House, and author of
The Ancient Language of Eden

During the many years I've known S. J., he has constantly inspired and motivated me to realize the Father's heart for us is intimacy with Him and living in His love. While reading this book, I was encouraged with that same precious insight into the character of our Father, and I believe you will be too.

Steve Wise
AMA Hall of Fame Inductee:
Professional Motorcycle Racing Champion and minister

WHAT'S GOD **REALLY** LIKE?

Unique Insights Into His Fascinating Personality

S. J. HILL

Energion Publications
Gonzalez, FL
2018

ISBN13: 978-1-63199-496-8
Library of Congress Control Number: 2018935549
Energion Publications - P. O. Box 841 - Gonzalez, FL 32560
energion.com
pubs@energion.com

Visit the author's website at www.sjhillonline.com. He can also be contacted at stephenhill6@gmail.com.

TABLE OF CONTENTS

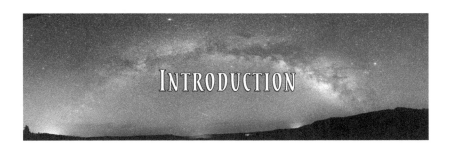

Anumber of years ago, I had the opportunity to be on the faculty of a ministry training school. One of the courses I taught was entitled *Cultivating Intimacy with God.* The primary purpose of the class was to introduce the students to the reality of God's extravagant love for them. The course was also designed to help them experience God as their Father and learn to enjoy Him out of an understanding of His enjoyment of them.

I'll never forget a conversation I had with a student at the end of one particular semester. A young woman approached me the last day of the course and said, "S. J., if I've learned anything in your class, I've discovered that God is *cool*." I don't know what kind of response she expected from me, but without any hesitation I said, "You're exactly right—God is *cool*! I just wish more of His children knew it."

The moment the words escaped from my mouth, I instinctively knew that if "certain Christians" had heard me, they would've been deeply troubled by what I had just said. More than likely, they would've chided me for using a common *slang* word in referring to God. But the more I've thought about what this young woman said, the more I've become convinced that she was right. She wasn't meaning to be disrespectful; instead, there were things said in my class that had opened her heart to God's personality and His extravagant affections for her. For the first time in her life, she was able to picture Him smiling over her, celebrating who He had made her to be. She was enjoying the fact that she felt loved and accepted, and in trying to express what she was experiencing, all she could say was "*God is cool!*"

If I were to ask you to describe God, what words would you use? Would you even be able to imagine Him having an appealing personality? Maybe things you've heard over the years about His character have left you either scared, bored, or both. Maybe you've been taught that God is to be feared and not enjoyed. Or, for some reason, you have thought of Him as somewhat "static," the One who sits on a throne in eternity, unapproachable and devoid of any real passion. Maybe you've even come to view Him merely as an "authority figure" that keeps things in order and punishes those who disobey Him.

Over the centuries, Christian theologians have spent countless hours contemplating the nature of God. From their studies they have discovered a number of things about His character that they have felt were clearly revealed in the Scriptures. These *attributes* of God have come to be called *divine perfections*. While the list has varied, to some degree from one theologian to another, it usually has included the following: God is infinite, sovereign, holy, all-powerful (omnipotent), all-wise (omniscient), personally present everywhere (omnipresent), and immutable (unchangeable).

But as profound as these truths are, there are things about God's nature that have been clearly omitted from the traditional list. For example, what about His joy? Isn't joy an attribute? If He is love, then can't we assume that He loves joyfully? If God is holy, then can't we also believe that He's perfect in His beauty and splendor? What about His meekness and humility? And, shouldn't His creativity also be considered an attribute? For some reason, these aspects of God's nature, as well as others, have often been overlooked or ignored down through the centuries.

Years ago, I decided to study and reflect on the Scriptures for the primary purpose of gaining new insights into God's fascinating personality. From the moment I made that decision, my life has never been the same. I have become intrigued by God. I think about Him all the time. I often wonder what He's really like. At times, I find myself trying to fathom the infinite depths of the Lord's splendor and beauty. Yet, at other times, I simply imagine Him smiling at me. I picture Him laughing, leaping, and celebrating what His grace has accomplished in my life. I even ponder what His songs about me might sound like.

In my ongoing quest to know and experience God, I am discovering more and more that He really is *cool!* He's in a league all by Himself, yet He has stooped to make Himself available to us. He's unchanging in His character, but He's never boring. He's faithful, but He's also fun. He's "holy wild," but His love is always constant.

I want to invite you on a treasure hunt to discover aspects of God's personality that appear to be somewhat *hidden* in the Bible. It's as if God has placed "nuggets" of truth about Himself deep within the Scriptures, and He longs for you to "dig them up" so you can truly know Him more. God loves to be sought after! And it's the exploration of the mysteries of who He really is that will not only create in you a holy curiosity and awe, but will also combat boredom in your life. There is nothing you can experience that is more invigorating than having God reveal Himself to you.

God has created you to be excited and exhilarated by the revelation of who He is. He wants you to enjoy Him. You weren't created to be bored. Your heart was made to be *fascinated* by the many facets of His incredible personality. Your life was meant to be an adventure leading you into His heart. Although you and I will never fully comprehend the vastness of God's nature, why don't you join me in exploring the infinite splendor of the One who made us for Himself!

THE ONE WHO LAUGHED FIRST

In the year 1514, a document was printed in Venice, Italy, that claimed to be a description of Jesus by a man named Publius Lentulus. Lentulus was believed to have been the Roman procurator of Judea around the time of Pontius Pilate. The Lentulus family was actually well known in the ancient Roman Empire, but Publius Lentulus never existed except in the mind of an eccentric individual who wanted to "pull the wool over the eyes" of the people of Europe.

Although the document was later discovered to be fraudulent, its influence throughout Europe and other parts of the world can't begin to be measured. The writing was called *The Epistle of Lentulus to the Roman Senate,* and it allegedly contained information about Jesus that one would not find in the four gospels. For example, the Lord was described as,

> ...a tall man, well shaped and of an amiable and revered aspect; his hair is of a color that can hardly be matched, falling into graceful curls...parted on the crown of his head, running as a stream to the front after the fashion of the Nazarenes; his forehead high, large and imposing; his cheeks without spot or wrinkle, beautiful with a lovely red; his nose and mouth formed with exquisite symmetry; his beard, of a color suitable to his hair, reaching below his chin and parted in the middle like a fork; his eyes bright blue, clear and serene....[1]

---

1   The published English translation of the Lentulus document does not mention a date or a translator. The original Italian version is also in the Library of Congress. I first read of this document in Sherwood E. Wirt's book, *Jesus, Man of Joy,* (Eugene, OR: Harvest House, 1999), 33-34.

In the very next paragraph there was a statement written that has left an indelible mark on humanity. Speaking of Jesus, it read, "No man has seen him laugh." This one comment alone went a long way in blinding Europe and a segment of the world to the beauty, joy, and smile of the most loving Man who ever lived.

Think of the so-called portraits of Jesus you've seen over the years. Most artists have either portrayed Him as stern, resolute, and somber, or they've depicted Him solely as the suffering Servant. But the real personality of Jesus has seldom come through in these representations of Him.

What's even more disheartening is that over the centuries, the Church has become deaf to the *laughter* of God. As a result, we have produced a morbid brand of Christianity that appears deathly boring and unattractive. The *good news* has been so overshadowed by the legalists and lovers of rules and regulations that for many people, either the Christian life is beyond their grasp or God is simply not desirable at all.

Yet nothing could be farther from the truth. God isn't anything like what so many of our images have portrayed Him to be. In fact, if you will venture with me into the pages of the Bible, I will take you on a journey that will help you capture the sights and sounds of the joyful God.

CELEBRATING CREATION

As we step back in time to the beginning of creation, we need to imagine the Lord more at play than at work. It appears that He thoroughly enjoyed Himself as He continually affirmed the goodness of all He had made (Genesis 1:31). He must have been overcome with absolute delight concerning the outcome. This appears to be what was at the heart of Robert Morris's translation of Proverbs 8:30-31: "I was by God's side, a master craftsman, delighting him day after day, ever at play before God's face, at play everywhere in God's world, sporting with the children of earth."[2]

2   Morris, Robert C. "God at Play in the World," *Weavings*, November-
     December 1994, 7.

These verses vividly describe *Wisdom* (the pre-incarnate Son of God) being actively involved in creation (See Colossians 1:16.). Yet, the scene is not of *someone* hard at work; it's a picture of *someone* hard at play!

Job 38:7 also informs us that when the foundations of the earth were laid, the morning stars sang together, and all the angels shouted for joy. When I first reflected on this verse, I found myself asking: "From *whom* were the angels taking their cue?" If God is eternally somber, the atmosphere certainly would not have been conducive for such an extravagant celebration!

While many choose to believe the universe began with a big bang, the worlds appear to have been created by a big, celebratory *shout*! God didn't speak the worlds into existence in a dull monotone. He was rejoicing in what He was doing and delighting in His creation. This is confirmed for us by the words of John in Revelation 4:11: "'You are worthy, O Lord our God, to receive glory and honor and power. For you created everything, and it is for your *pleasure* that they exist and were created'" (NLT, italics added).

If we take this verse at face value, it's clear that God made the worlds out of nothing and brought them into existence; and He did all of this for His own pleasure. He didn't do it just to demonstrate His power; He did it for sheer *joy*. So now, when we read the first two chapters of Genesis, we can come away with the impression that God was actually having fun!

Imagine little children playing together. They're completely engrossed in what they're doing. One of them speaks up and says, "Let's do this," and off they go. After they've enjoyed creating their own make-believe world for a while, another child blurts out, "I know what we should do" and off they go again, dreaming up another imaginary world in which to amuse themselves.

The first chapter of Genesis has a similar feel to it. Picture the Father, Son, and Holy Spirit saying to each other, "Let's make light," and they speak it into existence. The light is then separated from the darkness, and the two individual entities are called day and night. Then off they go again, their perfect imaginations in full swing. They divide the waters above from the waters below and call it heaven. Then they separate the waters below from the land and call them earth and sea. From there, they create plants and trees, the sun and moon, birds and creatures of the sea, as well as land creatures. Things continue to crescendo until creation reaches a climax with the making of a man and a woman.

Even when God did "rest" on the seventh day of creation, it wasn't because He was exhausted from all the activity and work. Instead, He wanted to pause and reflect on all He had made. He wanted to experience the *pleasure* of His handiwork and *celebrate* the love of the two people He had created. His was the rest of true satisfaction and joy!

THE FESTIVE GOD

As we continue our journey through the Scriptures, it soon becomes apparent that after creation, something went terribly wrong. The first couple turned their backs on the One who cared for them infinitely, and the perfect love story became the greatest human tragedy of all time. Yet, even in the face of man's rebellion, God refused to allow their bad choices to silence His joy and laughter. He provided redemption for man, and the door swung wide open for festive fellowship.

To further celebrate His redemptive joy and laughter, God initiated various festivals for His people to observe. These events were not about fasting, but rather about feasting. In fact, one of the Hebrew names for *festival* comes from a verb which means "to dance." The feasts were joyous occasions, characterized by singing, shouting, eating, and dancing.

For example, there were very few feasts that were as joyful as the week-long harvest Feast of Tabernacles (Booths). While this was a time for the Jews to celebrate God's blessings from the previous year, the Feast of Booths was primarily designed to remember the wilderness journey from Egypt to Canaan when God made the people live in booths (Leviticus 23:33-43). During the time of the

Feast, each Jewish family was supposed to build a booth, or *Sukkah*, and live in it for a week. Living in the small, temporary shelters was to be a tangible reminder of God's provision for them during their stay in the wilderness. Celebrating the Feast of Booths was a way for the people to express their joy over God's abundant blessings in their lives (Deuteronomy 16:15).

With the Sabbath observance, the Jewish people again were reminded and encouraged to celebrate God extravagantly! Rest from work was not the primary focus of the day. The Sabbath was to be a time for Israel to *rejoice* in the Lord and the life He had given them. The prophet Isaiah actually spoke of the Sabbath as a day of "delight" (Isaiah 58:13). Mourning and fasting were forbidden. Special festive white clothes were to be worn, and joyous music was to permeate the atmosphere. The Sabbath was to be regarded as a day in which Israel was to rest in the security of God's love and to live life to the fullest. The Lord wanted His people to be a reflection of His joy so they would become known around the world for their cheerfulness and laughter.

Throughout the Scriptures, God's people are continually encouraged to join in the festivity and laughter of heaven. In the Psalms alone, one can find over 100 various forms of the words joy, joyous, enjoy, gladness, delight, and jubilation. Although some of us may think a large portion of the Psalms *primarily* illustrate the hardships and struggles of life, nothing could be farther from the truth. More than anything else, they are songs of triumph and thanksgiving that communicate celebration and joy.

Listen to the chorus of psalmists who appear to have gotten caught up in something that's out of this world. "Clap your hands, all you nations; shout to God with cries of joy" (Psalm 47:1). "Sing joyfully to the LORD, you righteous; it is fitting for the upright to praise him" (Psalm 33:1).

> *Praise the LORD. Praise the LORD from the heavens, praise him in the heights above. Praise him, all His angels, praise him, all his heavenly hosts. Praise him, sun and moon,*

praise him, all you shining stars. Praise him, you highest heavens and you waters above the skies. Let them praise the name of the LORD, for he commanded and they were created (Psalm 148:1-5).

Praise him with the sounding of the trumpet, praise him with the harp and lyre, praise him with the tambourine and dancing, praise him with the strings and flute, praise him with the clash of cymbals, praise him with resounding cymbals (Psalm 150:3-5).

The sounds of celebration continue to echo throughout the pages of the Old Testament. God, through the prophet Isaiah, declared, "Sing for joy, O heavens, for the LORD has done this; shout aloud, O earth beneath. Burst into song, you mountains, you forests and all your trees, for the LORD has redeemed Jacob and displays his glory in Israel" (Isaiah 44:23). To Israel, the joyful God promised, "You will be a joy to all generations, *for I will make you so*" (Isaiah 60:15, NLT, italics added).

After Israel returned to Jerusalem following the Babylonian captivity, the Lord reminded them that *His joy* would be their strength (Nehemiah 8:10). The prophet Jeremiah also reassured the Jewish people that

The LORD will pay for the people of Jacob and will buy them back from people stronger than they were. The people of Israel will come to the high points of Jerusalem and shout for joy. Their faces will shine with happiness about all the good things from the LORD ... (Jeremiah 31:11-12, NCV).

The prophet Zephaniah even went so far as to write, "The LORD your God is with you, he is mighty to save. He will take great delight in you, he will quiet you with his love, he will rejoice over you with singing" (Zephaniah 3:17).

The Moffatt Bible, translated from the original languages by the Scottish scholar James Moffatt, contains eight verses from the

Psalms in which God is depicted as *smiling*. For example, this is vividly illustrated for us in Psalm 31:16:

> Smile *on thy servant, in thy love succor me.*

This truth is further reinforced for us in several other verses:

> *How precious is thy love, O God ... in thy* smile *we have the light of life* (Psalm 36:9).

> *O God, bless us with thy favor, may thy face* smile *on us* (Psalm 67:1).

> Smile *on thy servant, teach thy laws to me* (Psalm 119:135).

Moffatt took the various references to God's "shining face" found in the King James translation and turned them into *smiles*. Why should this surprise us or even shock us? Spurrell's translation of the Hebrew text also uses the word "smile" in the same verses. When thinking about the joy of the Lord, what better picture could be painted for us than one in which God is smiling?

It's sad, however, that there are those today who believe the language found in the preceding verses is simply to be taken figuratively. They will even argue that we should not attribute any human characteristics to God (technically known as anthropomorphism). Because God is Spirit, they will not allow themselves to imagine Him smiling, laughing, and shouting for joy. Yet many of these same individuals think that God is perpetually angry, wrathful, and hard to please.

This thinking stands out in stark contrast to the writers of the Westminster Shorter Catechism who, in contemplating the reason for man's existence, concluded that "the chief end of man is to glorify God and to enjoy Him forever." How can we honestly enjoy *someone* who doesn't smile and laugh? And since eternity is filled with everlasting joy, why do we automatically assume that the saints and angelic hosts are the only ones who are celebrating?

Why is it so difficult for us to believe that the *Lord of joy* is the One initiating the laughter?

A number of years ago, my sister-in-law prayed for a high school friend to encounter God's love in a personal way. Kathy continued to talk to him about Jesus, and he eventually opened his heart to the Lord and later became the worship leader for a local congregation. On the same day he experienced the Lord's love for the first time, Kathy had a vision in which she saw the angels leaping for joy. However, she also noticed *someone* in the midst of the angels jumping higher than all the others. As she looked closer at what was unfolding before her, she realized that the *One* who was celebrating the most was Jesus Himself.

While I certainly wouldn't encourage anyone to base their beliefs on another person's dreams and visions, why should Kathy's experience surprise us? If the angels celebrate when someone is ushered into the kingdom of God (Luke 15:10), why can't we believe that the One who died for mankind would also be the One who would celebrate the most?

LEARNING TO LAUGH WITH GOD

It took me a long time to imagine God laughing, but once I did, it began changing my outlook completely. I abandoned my drab perceptions of God, and I started picturing Him rejoicing over my life. Over the years, I've continued to learn to see things from His perspective. I've even found myself laughing more with Him, regardless of my circumstances. Maybe this is what Tertullian, an early Church father, was referring to when he wrote, "The Christian saint is hilarious."

If the *Lord of joy* lives in us, then we can join in His laughter. Since we, as followers of Christ, have been gifted with God-given insights into life, we can experience His smile, irrespective of our surroundings. This is one of the primary things that should characterize our lives in a world gripped by disappointment, heartache, and sadness.

The laughter of God should be a great source of hope and comfort to us. Since He can laugh at surmounting obstacles, we can feel secure. And this is the assurance that the Lord wanted to give the Hebrew slaves as He delivered them from the oppressive grip of Egypt. The people marched out of their captivity, freed by the blood of a *lamb*, and strengthened for the journey by feeding on a *lamb*. It was a great deliverance, but the plot was just beginning to thicken.

Even though Pharaoh had allowed Israel to leave Egypt, the Lord understood the ruler's heart. He knew that Pharaoh would regret his decision and assemble his army to overtake and overwhelm the Hebrew people. But little did Pharaoh know that God would let the ruler reveal his audacious arrogance and hardness of heart in order to ultimately free Israel from the tyranny of Egypt.

Still, the Hebrew people would have to go through a frightening ordeal. The Red Sea was in front of them, the Egyptian army was behind them, and the desert was on each side. The Israelites were certainly not in an enviable position. To them, the situation looked impossible. But they didn't realize that God would bring redemption out of the evil choices of Pharaoh, and they would experience freedom out of chaos.

A latent fear of Pharaoh had tormented the hearts and minds of the Hebrew people for years. Even after their deliverance from the land of Egypt, they found themselves terrified by the pursuit of Pharaoh's army. They said to Moses,

> *'Was it because there were no graves in Egypt that you brought us to the desert to die? What have you done to us by bringing us out of Egypt? Didn't we say to you in Egypt, Leave us alone; let us serve the Egyptians? It would have been better for us to serve the Egyptians than to die in the desert!'* (Exodus 14:11-12).

The Israelites didn't understand that they needed to face this crisis in order to experience a complete deliverance from the *fear* of Pharaoh and the Egyptians. But the Lord knew what had been haunting His people for years, so He instructed them to *go forward* (Exodus 14:15). What a challenge it must have been for them, especially when it *appeared* that the Lord had withdrawn His tangible, manifest presence from them. But ultimately Pharaoh's hatred and pursuit of the Hebrew people were actually used by the Lord to catapult Israel into the destiny He had for her.

What is the significance of all of this for us? The experience of the Hebrew people with Pharaoh should reinforce for us the fact that our heavenly Father will always turn *apparent* setbacks into safeguards, as well as dangers into divine destiny. This is why we need to see things from His perspective, laugh at our circumstances, and choose to remain unmoved in our trust of Him.

These same principles are also illustrated for us in the story of the three Hebrew boys who were thrown into a fiery furnace because they would not bow down and worship the golden image King Nebuchadnezzar had made (Daniel 3:27-30). What was meant to destroy Shadrach, Meshach, and Abednego actually became a place of protection. When the three boys stepped out of the perilous furnace with not even the smell of smoke on their garments, they immediately stepped into a place of promotion.

We even see these truths reenacted in the life of Daniel. A plot was devised by the governors of the land to try to kill Daniel because they were jealous of him. Daniel had distinguished himself from all the administrators in Darius' kingdom, and the king was thinking about placing Daniel over his whole realm. The governors began flattering Darius and eventually got him to sign a written decree stating that any man who prayed to any other "god" except him would be cast into a den of lions.

When the governors caught Daniel praying to the true God, they brought him before Darius and accused him of disobeying the law of the land. Even though the king loved Daniel deeply, he was forced by his own written decree to throw him into a den of lions. But instead of being eaten by the lions, Daniel was nurtured and sustained by the Lord. In fact, the lions' den became a safe haven and shelter from all of his accusers. When Daniel was eventually delivered from the "jaws of death," the king prospered him above all others (Daniel 6:28). Daniel went from *prison* to *promotion*, and those who had plotted to kill him were thrown into the same lions' den and devoured.

From these examples, we are reminded that even in the most trying circumstances God calls us to always see things from His perspective. However, the temptation for us in the face of impossible odds is to question God's faithfulness, especially when it seems that He has withdrawn His tangible presence from us. What complicates matters even more is that sometimes God *appears* to take an adversarial position against us. Some of the struggles we encounter seem to be struggles with the Lord. But the apparent "adversarial relationship" is in appearance only and is not reality!

It's during such seasons that we have to exhibit, as Brennan Manning suggests, a "ruthless trust." When we've prayed and cried to God for deliverance and still find ourselves no better off, God's character and commitment must sustain us.

While I certainly don't want to appear glib or offer shallow explanations about life's complex issues, *ruthless trust* will ultimately triumph over all suffering. In the face of adversity, faith says, "You can try to torment me, discourage me, and even make me cry, but you will not defeat me. You will not have the last word. I will outlast you and overcome you! I will join in the laughter of the One who loves me infinitely and chose me for Himself."

The story of Job certainly reinforces for us the power of a *ruthless trust*. This weak, lonely, broken man made it clear to all of us that we can stand with God when all the odds are against us. Although there may have been times we thought suffering and adversity could make us give up on everything, Job's relentless faith in God encourages us to believe even more that the One we love and serve will have the final say. Job's triumph over adversity is our triumph! His *ruthless trust* says to us that by our Father's abounding grace, we are up to the challenge.

It was this same *ruthless trust* that was also clearly demonstrated by the prophet Habakkuk. When local "thugs" were getting away with murder, and the world around him seemed to be going mad, Habakkuk asked God about it.

> *How long, O LORD, must I call for help, but you do not listen? Or cry out to you, 'Violence!' but you do not save? Why do you make me look at injustice? Why do you tolerate wrong? Destruction and violence are before me; there is strife, and conflict abounds. Therefore the law is paralyzed, and justice never prevails. The wicked hem in the righteous, so that justice is perverted* (Habakkuk 1:2-4).

In his wildest dreams, the prophet would not have expected the answer God gave him. The Lord told Habakkuk that the local "mobsters" were going to be replaced by "international warlords" who were even worse (vs. 5-7). In spite of God's response, Habakkuk pressed Him for more information. But while he waited for a response from the Lord, he did what was right. He didn't get cynical; he didn't desert God. He stood in his appointed place and waited. Habakkuk knew that those who trust in the Lord will ultimately not be disappointed.

Although the prophet was distressed beyond measure, he made one of the most powerful declarations of *ruthless trust* found in the Scriptures. With every ounce of strength he could muster, he boldly cried out,

> *Though the fig tree does not bud and there are no grapes on the vines, though the olive crop fails and the fields produce no food, though there are no sheep in the pen and no cattle in the stalls, yet I will rejoice in the LORD, I will be joyful in God my Savior. The Sovereign LORD is my strength; he makes my feet like the feet of a deer, he enables me to go on the heights* (Habakkuk 3:17-19).

Hezekiah chose to embrace the joy of God in spite of the devastating odds. He echoed heaven's perspective in spite of not having the answers to his questions. And it was his *ruthless trust* that reminds us again that even though we may not have all the answers to the perplexing questions that try to haunt us in times of suffering and adversity, we do know what our Father has done for us in Christ and that everything will ultimately work for our eternal good!

A SABBATH REST

[handwritten note in margin: The Sabbath is actually a gift of love. They never had a day off before this.]

When God led Israel into the wilderness, His people were exposed to howling winds and scorching heat, as well as frigid temperatures at night. But the Lord *defied* the desert by instituting the Sabbath in what appeared to be a *God-forsaken* place. And, He did it partly as a sign to Israel of their utter dependence upon Him for everything. They wouldn't get their food, water, or other provisions by their expertise or the sweat of their brow; instead, the Lord would instruct them to rest on the seventh day of the week as a visible, national declaration that the same God who created the world in six days would be the One who would provide everything for them in the wilderness.

Although Israel's observance of the Sabbath was required by the Lord, it was never meant to be a day of sadness as a result of arbitrary, religious regulations. As we've already seen, it was to be a day of joy with the reading of the Scriptures and a day of festivity celebrating life and love. The Sabbath rest was meant to symbolize a *joyful trust* that comes from knowing just how much the Lord infinitely loves and cares for those who are His!

The storyline of the Sabbath rest is needed as much now as ever before. In a world of economic turmoil, heartache and suffering, God wants to *defy* the "desert" of our human experience. In the midst of our fears and frustrations, as well as our worries and weaknesses, Father wants to remind us again that He will always provide. He is calling us to *rest* in His love and live out of His everlasting embrace. He is inviting us to join in His laughter against our *enemy*, and He is encouraging us to laugh with Him at our circumstances and celebrate the goodness of His heart!

LAUGHING AT THE IMPOSSIBLE

When the Lord appeared to Abraham and told him that his wife, Sarah, was going to conceive and give birth to a son and that by doing so she would become a mother of nations, Abraham "… fell on his face and laughed." Why did he laugh? Abraham laughed because he was 99 years old and Sarah was 90 (Genesis 17:17, NKJV).

It became even more interesting when three mysterious *visitors* appeared to Abraham and Sarah at their camp near the oaks of Mamre. There's no clear indication that Abraham knew who they were, but he treated them with extreme courtesy and hospitality. In the course of their conversation with Abraham, the guests inquired about Sarah's absence. Abraham explained to them that his wife was in a nearby tent. Having heard this, one of the visitors reiterated the promise God had given Abraham concerning the birth of his son. When Sarah heard the promise of a son, she laughed and said, "After I am worn out and my master is old, will I now have this pleasure?" (Genesis 18:12).

One of the guests heard Sarah's response and asked Abraham, "'Why did Sarah laugh…?'" And then, in a not so subtle way, the visitor reminded his hosts of the One who had made them the promise: "'Is anything too hard for the LORD? I will return to you at the appointed time next year and Sarah will have a son'" (v. 14).

Initially, Sarah tried to deny the fact that she had laughed (v. 15). But it was to no avail; the visitors had heard her response. Still, we have to believe they understood that underneath the laughter were years of unfulfilled expectations and a faith that had been reduced to a thread. Sarah's laugh was not only a brief protective response against being denied the promise, but it was also an uncontrollable expression of the hope she still carried in her heart. As was promised, the child of laughter (Isaac) was born the next spring. Sarah was able to say, "'God has brought me laughter, and everyone who hears about this will laugh with me'" (Genesis 21:6).

Abraham and Sarah's laughter has echoed down through the centuries as an encouragement to anyone who has struggled with the promises of God in the face of impossible odds. Their laughter should also be a reminder that the One who has made us the promises laughs at the impossibilities and offers us an eternal hope!

We, as followers of Christ, have every reason to laugh. The gospel invites us to laugh over the sealed fate of the kingdom of darkness; it challenges us to laugh at our problems in the presence of love; it beckons us to laugh at surprise outcomes of prayer; and, it compels us to laugh over the lost who have been brought home. Perhaps our most powerful weapons for saving the world are the laughter of God, the laughter of Christ's kingdom, and the laughter of death defeated and resurrection begun.

Maybe this is what Michael Yaconelli meant in his book, *Dangerous Wonder*:

> Instead of Christians wearing sackcloth and ashes at the condition of our world, maybe we should strike up a game of capture the flag in our neighborhood. Our neighbors need Jesus, but first they need a rousing evening of charades. Certainly our children need discipline, but what they may need more is a family Ping-Pong championship. What if our strategy to win the world was to "play" people into the kingdom of God? What if we invited people over to our home and, instead of telling them about our joy, lived it by playing with them? What if we could hear laughter in a church as well as "amens"?[3]

---

3   Yaconelli, Michael. *Dangerous Wonder* (Colorado Springs, CO: NavPress, 1998), 72.

In the National Art Gallery in London is a painting by Sandro Botticelli called *Mystic Nativity*. The obvious focal point of the painting is the baby Jesus, but what makes the scene so unusual is what is taking place outside the modest stable. Angels are dancing everywhere—around the stable, on the roof, and in the skies above! Botticelli's painting is extraordinary in that it depicts an extravagant universal joy!

The *good news* of Jesus' birth was an invitation to the world to come back to the Father's embrace; it was a call to come back to *joy*! Why else would the angel say to the shepherds, "'Do not be afraid. I bring you good news of great joy that will be for all the people'" (Luke 2:10)? Luke even tells us that a multitude of heavenly hosts appeared with the angel announcing the birth of Christ with a choral celebration of praise (vs. 13-14).

A KINGDOM OF JOY

With the birth of God's Son, a kingdom would also be born that would be established on *joy*! Although the birth of Jesus would be an extremely costly event for Mary and Joseph, they were willing to endure severe personal hardship because they had been visited by an angelic messenger who had brought them *good news* that would forever change the face of humanity. The personal embarrassment that came with Mary's "out of wedlock" pregnancy, the couple's taxing and tiring journey from Nazareth to Bethlehem just prior to the delivery of the Baby Jesus, and the stigma associated with their child being born in a crude, smelly stable would all be overshadowed by ne sheer *joy* of introducing the long-awaited Messiah to a world that desperately needed to be embraced by a loving, laughing God!

The *Child* in Mary's womb would become the hope of the world and would "save his people from their sins" (Matthew 1:21). The *joy* contained in this promise was such that when Elizabeth was visited by her cousin, Mary, and was informed by the Holy Spirit that Mary would give birth to the Messiah, Elizabeth's unborn baby leaped inside her womb (Luke 1:41)! Mary was so overjoyed that she sang, "'My soul glorifies the Lord and my spirit rejoices in God my Savior'" (vs. 46-47). Mary and Joseph were willing to suffer the stigma of Jesus' birth because they had a lot to look forward to that would be "out of this world!"

The joy of God, revealed and celebrated in the Nativity, was also seen and experienced throughout the life and ministry of Jesus. The first chapter of the Book of Hebrews gives us a unique insight into why the Lord had such an appealing personality. According to verse nine, Jesus had been anointed by His Father with the oil of *gladness* above His companions.

Could this have been one of the primary reasons why the Galilean fishermen left their nets and followed Christ? Or what about Levi the tax collector who deserted his money box to join the Lord's revolutionary cause? Jesus was a man of such joy and freedom that He was irresistible to many people. They wanted to be close to Him to catch His contagious spirit and to share in His joy so they could participate in the celebration of His coming kingdom.

Picture for a moment the way Jesus conducted Himself around children as He allowed them to jump into His lap, tug on His beard, and kiss Him. Jesus even rebuked His disciples for being spoilsports when they attempted to put a damper on all the fun.

This was the same glad-hearted Jesus who allowed women and those of other cultures and races to get close to Him. Although He was *someone* who would become familiar with rejection and sorrow, He was such a Man of compassion and *joy* that people knew they would always be treated with love and respect.

Think of the first miracle that Jesus ever performed (John 2:1-11). It occurred at a wedding of all places. Jesus and His mother were among the invited guests, along with the disciples. To fully appreciate what took place at the wedding ceremony in Cana of Galilee, we need to see Jesus for who He really is—a *cheerful Man*! While this may be difficult for some of us to imagine because of all the somber depictions of Him that have been portrayed by religious tradition, it's quite apparent from what happened that Jesus enjoyed a good party!

During the time of Christ, it was customary at social festivities to have the best wine served first. As things progressed throughout the next few days, a very cheap grade of wine would be offered to those who kept coming back for more. In stark contrast, Jesus did just the opposite. With His first miracle, He introduced the best wine toward the end of the celebration. Quite possibly He did it to honor the bride and groom. But whatever His reason was, He did it to the amazement of everyone!

The Gospel of John also informs us that Jesus turned the water into wine as a *sign* to the wedding party and their guests. But, what exactly did the miracle signify? Maybe it was symbolic of the life of joy that would be experienced by those who would embrace Christ's message. Or, perhaps the miracle pointed to the Day of Pentecost, a time when the Holy Spirit would be *poured out* on many and they would come to know the *joy* and *exhilaration* of being filled to overflowing! But one thing we do know is that when Jesus turned the water into wine, He was giving us a glimpse into what it would be like at His own wedding when He would again save the *best wine* for last (Revelation 19:7-9).

A MESSAGE AND MINISTRY OF JOY

After Jesus had taught extensively throughout Galilee and word of His ministry had spread like wildfire, He returned to Capernaum with His disciples. When He discovered that the crowds were larger than ever, He hiked up the side of a mountain to a favorite spot, sat down, and began teaching the people. What immediately came out of His mouth was an incredibly inspiring message of *joy* that later came to be known as the Sermon on the Mount.

As we turn the pages of the New Testament to the Beatitudes (Matthew 5:3-10), we find that the very first word Jesus spoke was "Blessed," a term derived from the Greek word *makarios*. In commenting on the meaning of the word *makarios*, William Barclay wrote:

> The blessedness which belongs to the Christian is not a blessedness which is postponed to some future world of glory; it is a blessedness which exists here and now. It is not something into which the Christian will enter; it is something into which he (or she) has entered. It is a present reality to be enjoyed. The Beatitudes say in effect, "O the bliss of being a Christian! O the sheer happiness of knowing Jesus Christ as Master, Savior, and Lord!" The very form of the Beatitudes is the statement of the joyous thrill and the radiant gladness of the Christian life. In the face of the Beatitudes a gloom-encompassed Christianity is unthinkable.
>
> Makarios then describes that joy which has its secret within itself, that joy which is serene and untouchable and self-contained, that joy which is completely independent of all the chances and changes of life. The Beatitudes speak of that joy which seeks us through our pain, that joy which sorrow and loss, pain and grief are powerless to touch, that joy which shines through tears, and which nothing in life or death can take away.
>
> The world can win its joys and the world can equally well lose its joys. But the Christian has the joy which comes from walking forever in the company and in the presence of Jesus Christ. The Beatitudes are triumphant shouts of bliss for a permanent joy that nothing in the world can ever take away.[4]

What Jesus was actually talking about in the Beatitudes was a deep, profound *joy* that would be experienced by those who chose

---

4   Barclay, William. *The Daily Study Bible: The Gospel of Matthew*, vol. 1 (Edinburgh: The Saint Andrew Press), 83-85.

to partake in the salvation of His kingdom. But to better understand the real meaning of what Jesus said, we need to change the
language of the verses just slightly. Let's see how the Beatitudes
would read with a little different wording:

Joyful are the poor in spirit,
*   for theirs is the kingdom of heaven.*
Joyful are those who mourn, for they shall be comforted.
Joyful are the meek, for they shall inherit the earth.
Joyful are those who hunger and thirst for righteousness,
*   for they shall be filled.*
Joyful are the merciful, for they shall obtain mercy.
Joyful are the pure in heart, for they shall see God.
Joyful are the peacemakers,
*   for they shall be called children of God.*
Joyful are those who are persecuted for righteousness' sake,
*   for theirs is the kingdom of heaven.*

Notice how the Beatitudes come alive with fresh, new meaning!
Instead of merely viewing them as rewards for spiritual achieve-
ments, we can now see them as "joy-filled" promises given to those
who share in the realities of God's kingdom.

Even the stories that Jesus told brought joy to those who had
little reason to be happy. One such story was about a man who
decided to have an extravagant feast and invite all of his friends
(Luke 14:16-24). The dinner invitations were delivered, and a large
amount of money was spent on food and entertainment. The day
of the feast arrived, and the host sent his servant to announce to
the guests that it was time for the party to begin.

However, instead of the guests beating a path to their friend's
house, it appears that every one of them had better things to do.
One of them said to the servant, "I have bought a piece of ground,
and I must go and see it. I ask that you have me excused." Jesus'
audience was probably thinking to themselves, "Why would this
invited guest rather look at a piece of land than participate in what
is going to be the ultimate party?"

Another guest said to the servant, "I have bought five yokes of oxen, and I am going to test them. I ask you to have me excused." By now, the listeners were possibly thinking that these invited guests were out of their minds!

A third invitee then came up with probably the best excuse of them all: "I have married a wife, and therefore I cannot come." At this point, the people listening to Jesus had to be beside themselves.

Jesus then proceeded to tell His listeners what the host of the party did. He sent his servant into the streets and lanes of the city and told him to bring to the feast those who were poor, crippled, blind, and lame. After the servant had completed his mission, there was still room for more guests. So the host said, "'Go out to the roads and country lanes, and make them come in, so that my house will be full. I tell you, not one of those men who were invited will get a taste of my banquet'" (vs. 23-24).

As Jesus finished the punch line of the story, those around Him must have been stunned. The self-righteous bigots who had been listening to Christ probably began to wonder if the story was, in some strange way, really about them. And, if true, how could they stand by and do nothing while He was undermining their "good standing" in the religious community?

Although these men were certainly not happy with what Jesus was clearly implying in His storyline, there must have been joy and laughter in heaven. Yet, it was laughter of a different kind. It was joy over the kingdom of God coming to earth; it was laughter that was expressed on behalf of the poor, the crippled, the blind, the lame, and the outcasts who had been shunned by the religious system. The *excluded* would now be *included,* and heaven would join in the celebration!

The celebration would continue as Jesus sent out 70 disciples to declare and demonstrate the *good news* of the kingdom to the cities and towns He intended to visit. When these men returned from their travels, they were filled with *joy* over what they had experienced. Were they laughing? Of course they were laughing! They were elated because they were participants in the advancement of the kingdom of God and that even the demons were subject to them.

Apparently the 70 weren't the only ones laughing. In later writing about the event, Luke captured in words one of the most priceless scenes that would ever be recorded about Jesus. Notice the language very carefully:

> *At that time Jesus, full of* joy *through the Holy Spirit, said, 'I praise you, Father, Lord of heaven and earth, because you have hidden these things from the wise and learned, and revealed them to little children. Yes, Father, for this was your good pleasure'* (Luke 10: 17-21, italics added).

The *extravagant joy* that Jesus modeled in His message and ministry has been beautifully illustrated in the words of Michael McIntosh:

> The joy of the Lord was at the tomb of the resurrected Lazarus, overshadowing the sadness and disappointment of the dead man's sisters. Joy was there when the leper returned to thank Jesus. Joy was there when a woman caught in the very act of adultery was forgiven and released from her sin. Joy was there when the deaf heard, the blind saw, and the lame walked. Joy was there on the mountainside as the multitudes listened to the profound teachings of Jesus. Joy was there when the little children flocked to Jesus. Joy was there when the boy gave Jesus his lunch so that He could work a miracle and feed the thousands. Joy was there when Jesus forgave Zacchaeus for abusing his authority. Joy was there when Jesus stood up in the boat and stopped the storm. Joy was there when dawn broke and the women knew that Jesus was resurrected from the dead. Everywhere Jesus went, joy tagged along.[5]

---

5   MacIntosh, Dr. Michael K. *The Tender Touch of God* (Eugene, OR: Harvest House, 1996), 200.

THE HUMOR OF JESUS

Although it may be difficult for some of us to imagine Jesus smiling and laughing, the more we explore the gospels, the more it should be obvious that He had a real sense of humor! Judge for yourself—Jesus painted a somewhat humorous word picture for His listeners when He taught that it would be easier for a camel to go through the eye of a needle than for a rich man to enter the kingdom of God. He vividly described the painstaking care with which the religious leaders washed the outside of their cups before drinking from them, but left the inside dirty. He even spoke of the Jewish teachers of the Law as those who strained at gnats and swallowed camels!

Consider the story of the Canaanite woman who begged Jesus to heal her daughter. Using a familiar analogy, "He replied, 'It is not right to take the children's bread and toss it to the dogs'" (Matthew 15:26). On the surface, the way Jesus reacted to the woman appears callous and out of character. His apparent reluctance to respond to her in love is rather shocking since the gospel accounts describe Jesus as one who readily showed mercy to those who were in need, regardless of their nationality or gender.

Although Jesus eventually healed the woman's daughter, why did He appear to treat her in a very uncaring way? Some commentators have suggested that He was testing her faith. Apparently, Jewish rabbis often turned down requests from would-be students three times in order to test their resolve. But in Matthew's account, Jesus seemed to go beyond that. He appeared to flatly reject her because she was a Canaanite, "a dog!"

However, I believe there is a better way to understand what Jesus was doing. In reading the surrounding verses, it's obvious that Jesus wasn't testing the faith of the Canaanite woman; He was testing the hearts of His disciples. I propose Jesus was using satire to point out to His disciples that they still didn't understand what He had been teaching them concerning the importance of the attitudes of one's heart, as opposed to merely adhering to the traditions of men.[6]

Satire was frequently used in the Greco-Roman world as a way of applying *humor*, irony, and exaggeration to different situations in order to expose people's wrong beliefs and attitudes. Just prior to Jesus' encounter with the Canaanite woman, some scribes and Pharisees had questioned Jesus about His disciples not washing their hands before they ate (vs. 1-2). The religious leaders weren't interested in hygiene; they were concerned with ritual cleanliness and purity codes—identity markers (things like what they ate and how they dressed) that kept them separate from Gentiles.

Jesus used the opportunity to teach His disciples about what truly made a person clean (undefiled) or unclean (defiled). Jesus was trying to expand the thinking of His disciples about the importance of what they harbored in their hearts; whatever was there would eventually be revealed through their words, whether clean or unclean (vs. 10-20). And, it was in this context that Jesus encountered the Canaanite woman.

When the woman initially approached Jesus, He didn't immediately answer her because, I believe, He was waiting to see what His disciples would do and what would come out of their mouths. He was testing their attitudes to determine whether they had understood what he had just been teaching them.

But what came out of their mouths? "Send her away, for she keeps crying out after us" (v. 23). The disciples revealed what was in their hearts. They still saw Canaanites the way the scribes and Pharisees did. They still believed Gentiles were unclean and defiled because of what they ate, even though Jesus had just taught them otherwise.

At this point, Jesus could've corrected his disciples for misunderstanding what they had just been taught, but I believe he took a different approach. He began using satire to make a more

---

6   The thoughts in the section on Jesus' encounter with the Canaanite woman were inspired by Russ Hewett's blog post entitled, *How Jesus Used Satire to Teach His Disciples*, August 20, 2017: www.meetingplace.church.

lasting impression. Picture Jesus turning toward His disciples and apparently *adopting* their merciless attitude and saying, "It is not right to take the children's bread and toss it to the dogs." He made it look like He agreed with His disciples by echoing the way they felt about the woman.

But the Canaanite woman responded "...Even the dogs eat the crumbs that fall from their master's table." Jesus was astonished by what he heard coming out of the woman's mouth. Her words actually revealed that her humility and attitude were far more God-like than those of His disciples. I believe at that moment, Jesus stopped using satire and said, "'... Woman, you have great faith! Your request is granted.' And her daughter was healed at that moment." Imagine the disciples' mouths dropping open as Jesus cleverly exposed their wrong attitudes and lack of understanding. I expect this lesson stayed with them for a very long time.

I think it's only fitting to suggest that when Jesus was dialoguing with the Canaanite woman, there was a *gleam* in His eye and a *smile* on His face. He was not only challenging the woman for a response (which was a common, cultural practice in Jesus' day), but He also was inviting her to experience the joy and celebration of His coming kingdom. Why should we assume anything else?

Again, think about the time Jesus came walking on the water to His disciples (Matthew 14:22-33). Why scare them out of their minds by walking up to their boat on the Sea of Galilee between three and four in the morning? I really think Jesus was having some fun at the disciples' expense! And, it didn't stop there. Imagine the disciples' response as Jesus admonished them to "not be afraid" as He was standing in front of them looking somewhat *ghost-like* while they were doing everything humanly possible not to sink with the ship!

Even in all of the accounts of feeding the 5,000, there seemed to be an undertone of *teasing* in the way Jesus addressed His disciples. For example, when they expressed concern that it was getting late and the people needed to be encouraged to go into the villages to buy food, notice Jesus' response. He looked at His disciples (probably with a twinkle in His eye) and said, "'…They do not need to go away. You give them something to eat'" (Matthew 14:16). Can you imagine the utter shock the disciples must have experienced as they heard those words and felt the weight of responsibility that accompanied them? However, when Jesus took the five loaves and two fish that had been given to the disciples and then multiplied the food, they must have felt relieved. But more than likely, they realized that Jesus was again having some fun at their expense!

THE JOY OF THE FATHER'S LOVE

While it's critical for our spiritual sanity to imagine Jesus as our joyful Savior and Friend, it's just as important for us to understand the source of His joy. Jesus' joy was derived from the warmth of His Father's love and tender affections. Furthermore, it was the Father's love that would sustain Him throughout His life.

Jesus was born into an "orphaned" planet and forced to deal with the deep, dark abyss of human existence.[7] Rejection and pain seemed to stalk Him from the very beginning. He was rumored to be the child of a *troubled,* teenage girl. The Scriptures also strongly suggest that there was nothing physically attractive about his appearance (Isaiah 53:2). Religious leaders thought he was demonized, and others called him a glutton and a drunkard. He was even rejected by members of His own family and eventually crucified as a common criminal.

Yet, the one thing that enabled Christ to deal with the emotional trauma He experienced was the love and approval of His heavenly Father! As a man, it was absolutely essential for Jesus to feel loved and affirmed by Him. This is why His Father, on a couple of different occasions, publicly proclaimed His love for His Son. For example, at the baptism of Jesus, His Father spoke these powerful words: "'…You are my Son, whom I love; with you I am

---

7   Parts of the section, **The Joy of the Father's Love**, are taken from a chapter entitled "The Crowning Glory of Our Lives" by S. J. Hill, in *Catching God's Heart*, compiled by Frank DeCenso Jr. (Shippensburg, PA: Destiny Image Publishers, 2010), 58-59, 61.

well pleased'" (Luke 3:22). This is how Christ began His ministry in Galilee. Before He had preached one message or performed one miracle, He heard and experienced a deeply profound affirmation from heaven. Yet, His Father's approval was not based on anything He had done or accomplished; instead, it was deeply rooted in the reality that He was uniquely loved by His Father and that they had a very special relationship with each other.

Again, at Christ's transfiguration (Matthew 17:5), the Father echoed the same words He had spoken at Jesus' baptism. It was these very words that would give Jesus the security He needed. The paramount passion of His life was His Father, and this would be the reason for His success in life and ministry.

Nevertheless, things would not be easy for the promised Messiah. His Sonship would constantly be called into question, and the adversary even tempted Him to "prove" He was God's Son. Jesus was challenged to turn stones into bread, throw Himself from the pinnacle of the temple to be caught by angels, and accept the accolades that would be due Him by embracing Satan's offer of the kingdoms of this world. Yet, Christ resisted the temptations to prove His Sonship; in fact, He knew He didn't have to prove anything because He lived out of His true identity as the *Beloved of the Father.*

Living Out of the Father's Smile

One of the primary reasons for Christ's mission to planet earth was to introduce us to His Father so we could experience the joy of being loved by Him (John 14:6; 17:3). He even reiterated this truth by suggesting that to see Him is to see the Father (John 14:9). Jesus also modeled for us a relationship between a *Father* and a *Son* in order that we could learn from His example and live free as Father's sons and daughters. In fact, this was the basis for His prayer in John 17: 22-23, 26:

> *'I have given them the glory that you gave me, that they*
> *may be one as we are one: I in them and you in me. May*

*they be brought to complete unity to let the world know that you sent me **and have loved them even as you have loved me**. I have made you known to them, and will continue to make you known in order that **the love you have for me may be in them and that I myself may be in them***' *(emphasis added).*

Still, the Father knew it would be difficult for us to grasp the measure of His love for us, so He chose to give us an incredible gift that would help us feel and experience the joy of being His sons and daughters (Luke 11:13). He sent the Holy Spirit to live within us and to constantly remind us of who we really are:

> *So, you should not be like cowering, fearful slaves. You should behave instead like God's very own children, adopted into his family—calling him 'Father, dear Father.' For his Holy Spirit speaks to us deep in our hearts and tells us that we are God's children* (Romans. 8:15-16, NLT).

The Holy Spirit is continually attempting to remind us that we are the Father's sons and daughters, not orphans. He is forever trying to drown out the accusing voice of the "father of lies" who always tries to suggest to us that we're unlovable. As the Spirit of Truth, He not only wants us to accept the fact that we are the Father's children, but He is doing everything He can to help us feel and experience what Jesus felt!

However, some of the biggest challenges we face concerning our identity as Father's children are due to deeply rooted negative images of ourselves and misconceptions about God's feelings for us. And these are battles that we all fight! The Apostle Paul described the struggles in very warlike terms:

> *The weapons we fight with are not the weapons of the world. On the contrary, they have divine power to demolish strongholds. We demolish arguments and every pretension that sets itself up against the knowledge of God, and we*

take captive every thought to make it obedient to Christ (2 Corinthians 10:4-5).

In the original Greek language, the word "arguments" means thoughts, reasonings, and imaginations that shape and affect our behavior. Thoughts and images about ourselves that make us feel like orphans, instead of our Father's children, can eventually become strongholds or fortresses from which rejection, insecurity, and fear will try to sabotage our lives. These strongholds can also include lies about who God really is and about His feelings for us.

Our minds will be influenced either by our Father's affirmations of us revealed in the Scriptures or by the negative thoughts and images that continually try to cripple us through feelings of rejection, loneliness, and shame. Often these thoughts and ungodly beliefs creep into our minds in such subtle ways that we don't even recognize them for what they are. They feel so personal that we accept them and end up thinking and acting like orphans.

Orphan thinking imagines God as a hard taskmaster who must always be appeased. It makes us believe that we have to pray more, read the Bible more, fast more, or work harder in order to earn His love and favor. It makes us observe various Christian disciplines more out of religious duty than delight. As a result, we rarely experience true inner peace and rest. Because our motivation is wrong, we easily get frustrated and seldom experience true intimacy with God.

Orphan thinking motivates us to live by "law" rather than *love*. We attempt to relate to God by adhering to certain rules and regulations. If we believe His love is conditional, we value outward obedience more than a loving relationship. As a result, God seems so far away because our hearts are unknowingly closed to intimacy.

Orphan thinking produces a low self-image that can lead to self-hatred and rejection. It encourages us to compare ourselves to others, which makes us feel even more unlovable. It causes us to believe that other people get all the breaks and are more blessed than we are. As a result, we continually struggle with feelings of abandonment and have a difficult time trusting in God's love for us.

Orphan thinking also drives us to seek the acceptance and attention of others. We long for the approval of our peers or even those we look up to as "father figures." Yet, we soon discover that the affection we are starving to experience is never really given to us. Instead, our need for approval only leads to more rejection and feelings of insignificance.

Orphan thinking even causes us to believe that we have to "have it all together" spiritually in order to be fully accepted by God and to avoid His judgment and wrath. Therefore, we live with an increasing sense of condemnation and shame because of our continual failure to *achieve* perfection.

Just as faulty thoughts and images about God can lead to the establishment of unhealthy strongholds in our personalities, a true understanding of Father's feelings for us can liberate us and enable us to continually live out of His smile. For example, Nehemiah 8:10 tells us that the *joy of the Lord* is our strength. The Hebrew word for *strength* can also be translated *stronghold*. When we imagine *God's joy* over us and His celebration of our lives, His affections for us will become a safe haven into which we can escape. Instead of running into various strongholds of addiction or getting involved in other activities to help deaden the pain when we're battling our "orphan issues," we can run into our Father's embrace and experience the joy and security of His love.

The more we look into the face of the joyful Jesus, the more we will be able to imagine the smile of the Father. And, it's the joy of the Father that will allow us to think and act as His sons and daughters. We will see God as *our* loving Father who accepts us unconditionally and whose love for us will never be based on anything we do for Him. Instead of striving to earn His approval, we will be able to rest in the fact that we are fully and completely loved in Christ and justified by His grace.

As sons and daughters, we will discover that certain "disciplines," such as prayer and meditating the Scriptures, will start to take on a whole new meaning for us. Instead of doing these things out of duty or fear, the *disciplines* will become a *delight* to us. We will find ourselves wanting to live life with our Father, as well as de-siring to spend times of solitude with Him, because we understand that He always loves being with us and He can't get enough of us!

As sons and daughters, we will desire to live free from habit-ual sin because of our love for our heavenly Father. When we're secure in His love, we won't want to hurt or grieve Him; we won't want anything to hinder our relationship with Him. We will want our lives to be places of rest for Him. As a result, instead of being motivated by fear and intimidation, the pleasure of our Father's unconditional love will become our primary motivation for purity.

And, as sons and daughters, we will feel loved and affirmed because we understand how valuable and special we are to our Fa-ther. Regardless of how many times we mess up, we will know for a certainty that Father will always be there for us. We will be able to pick ourselves up and keep running into His arms because we un-derstand He is more committed to us than we will ever be to Him!

3 THE DANCING DEITY

The whole world is enveloped in wonder! Embrace it through any one of your five senses, and you have a nonstop sequence of sensations that keep your brain bombarded and your nervous system spinning. Light waves inundate your eyes with rapid successions of color and shade; sound waves serenade your ears with an endless medley of pitches and rhythms; "touches that bring an abundant array of textures to our fingertips; tastes that reveal the rich essence of creation's vast cuisine; smells that unlock its permeating aromas."[8]

But our senses are often held captive by our wills and the limited expectations of our minds and imaginations. Because we're extremely selective, we primarily see, hear, smell, taste, and touch what we allow ourselves to experience. Our senses, if too carefully filtered, can even become somewhat predictable and dull, and we can gradually lose touch with this "wonder-filled" world. In the words of Robert Capon: "We are in a war between dullness and astonishment."[9]

Yet, what would happen if we all took Jesus' advice and became more childlike? What if we determined to live a life of *wonder* and *astonishment*? I believe it's time for us to rediscover creation around us and let it become a window to the beauty of God. I also believe it's time to be reintroduced to the One who is colorfully creative—the God who sculpts and paints, dances and sings, and does so

---

8   Needham, Phil. *He Who Laughed First* (Kansas City, MO: Beacon Hill Press, 2000), 36.

9   Capon, Robert Farrar. *The Astonished Heart* (Grand Rapids: Eerdmans, 1996), 120.

with consummate control, yet with adventurous abandon. God is never static! Neither is He the "Unmoved Mover" of the universe. He is the ultimate Artist who has surrounded us with a myriad of magnificent mysteries, and He beckons us to believe and explore.

While God is often described as Creator, how often is He depicted as the *Sculptor* of mountains and rivers and the *Designer* of the hippopotamus and the hummingbird? Though we celebrate His power in creation, how often do we overlook His intriguing inventiveness and passionate playfulness?

In her book, *Pilgrim at Tinker Creek*, Annie Dillard wrote of the unbridled splendor of God's creativity. As she journeyed in nature around her place in the Virginia Appalachians, she realized she was enveloped by something that was both wonderful and mysterious.

> The creator goes off on one wild, specific tangent after another, or millions simultaneously, with an exuberance that would seem to be unwarranted, and with an abandoned energy sprung from an unfathomable font. What is going on here? The point of the dragonfly's terrible lip, the giant water bug, birdsong, or the beautiful dazzle and flash of sunlighted minnows, is not that it all fits together like clockwork...but that it all flows so freely wild, like the creek, that it all surges in such a free, fringed tangle. Freedom is the world's water and weather, the world's nourishment freely given, its soil and sap: and the creator loves pizzazz.[10]

God's creativity is probably the most obvious thing about Him. He showcases it! He is continually exhibiting His crafts. But, in other ways, God's creativity is hidden. "Much of what He makes He tucks away, in microscopic minuteness or cosmic immensity, deep beneath us or far above us."[11] Still, He calls us to explore and

---

10 Dillard, Annie. *Pilgrim at Tinker Creek* (New York: Harper and Row, 1975), 137.

11 Buchanan, Mark. *The Holy Wild* (Sisters, OR: Multnomah Publishers, Inc., 2003), 176.

enjoy the vast expanse of His universal playground. What we're about to embark on is designed to leave us awestruck and amazed!

A HEAVENLY ART GALLERY

For far too long, the scope of Psalm 19:1 has escaped many of us. When David wrote, "The heavens declare the glory of God; the skies proclaim the work of his hands," he never imagined the possibilities that would await those of us who would be alive in the 21ˢᵗ century. What we have been given is an indescribable invitation to take a tour of a "heavenly gallery," displaying the most unimaginable, breathtaking art.

With breakthroughs in science and technology, each of us can now peer into the unfathomable depths of sky and space to behold the handiwork of the Artist. This is why we can no longer remain content with mere theological definitions that try to describe the nature and splendor of God. To simply believe that He is present throughout the universe and limitless in power can't be sufficient to satisfy our curiosity. While these truths may be theologically correct, they don't have the ability to take our breath away. No wonder our fascination with God may be somewhat limited!

The boundaries of our thinking may have also become way too narrow. This is why we really need some magnificent measurements and "out of this world" illustrations of God's infinity that will awaken our imaginations and capture our hearts. So let me, as your guide, invite you to take a journey to a far distant *place*. But, I must warn you—you'll definitely have to hold on to your seats!

As you begin the voyage, imagine the planets in your solar system having been sculptured by Father's *fingers* and splashed with a kaleidoscope of colors. While touring the galaxy, first marvel at Mercury covered in craters and colored in gray. Next, venture to Venus with its yellow and red hues. From there, make your way to Mars, a planet mysteriously masked in reddish, brown tones. Journey on to Jupiter and explore its breathtaking red, white, orange, and yellow bands. Then sail to Saturn and discover a planet sprinkled with a pale yellow hue and encircled by beautiful, intricate rings. Travel further to *unusual* Uranus and observe its painted, bluish green tones as it spins on its side around the Sun. Finally, navigate to Neptune and relish its rich blue color and eye-catching clouds.

While continuing your exploration, let me remind you that your solar system is part of a galaxy that is called the Milky Way. The Milky Way is approximately 100,000 light years in diameter.[12] In other words, if you could travel at the speed of light (186,000 miles a second), it would take you 100,000 years just to cross it from end to end.

Think about how many stars are in our galaxy alone. The human eye can only see about 4,000 stars under the best of conditions. The Milky Way contains approximately 200 billion stars! And we are only one galaxy among some 150 billion others, each with billions of stars.

To put this in perspective, the next time you're at the beach, grab a handful of sand. Then try to count each grain. It will be impossible! But if you were to take every single grain of sand from every beach on earth, you wouldn't come close to equaling the number of stars in the galaxies of the universe. And our Father made them all! What's even more amazing is He named all of them! The Psalmist declared, "He determines the number of the stars and calls them each by name" (Psalm 147:4). No wonder the next verse broadcasts these words: "Great is our Lord and mighty in power; his understanding has no limit" (v. 5).

The next time you have a chance to look at the stars on a clear night, pick out one that catches your eye. While it may appear to be somewhat close, the nearest star is a system of three called Alpha Centauri.[13] The closest of these is Proxima Centauri, a meager 4.25 light years away. Now, a light year is how far light travels in one calendar year. Since light moves at an astounding speed of 186,000

12 Facts taken from Sam Storms, *One Thing* (Scotland, Great Britain: Christian Focus Publications Ltd, 2004), 91-92.
13 Ibid., 89.

miles per second, that means it travels 670,000,000 miles an hour. So, if light moves at 670,000,000 miles an hour, it can travel six trillion miles (6,000,000,000,000) in a 365-day period. That's the equivalent of 12,000,000 round trips to the Moon.

The Hubble Space Telescope has also detected a distant galaxy that scientists estimate is approximately 13 billion light years from the earth.[14] Remember, a light year is six trillion miles. That would put this galaxy at 78 sextillion (78,000,000,000,000,000,000,000) miles from earth. And, astronomers tell us that the universe is still expanding.

If that didn't make your head swim, then try to wrap your mind around this—the sun is approximately 870,000 miles wide.[15] As stars go, it's rather small. But you could fit approximately 1,000,000 earths inside the sun! Speaking of the sun, you can wake up every morning with the assurance that mankind will never freeze to death because in the sun hundreds of billions (10 with 38 zeros) of fusion reactions take place every second. At its core, the sun's temperature is about 15 million degrees Celsius or approximately 27 million degrees Fahrenheit. 100,000,000,000 tons of dynamite would have to be detonated every second to match the energy produced by the sun. And this is only one sun among billions of trillions of others, all of which are the results of the sustaining power and energy of Jesus (Colossians 1:17).

DOWN TO EARTH

As you try to catch your breath and come back down to earth, observe with me the Artist actively at play, applying color on the canvas of the sky. With each passing day, He paints new patches of clouds and decorates the heavens with feathery fowl. Like an unconventional inventor, He keeps indulging Himself with innovations that come in a myriad of shapes and sizes. He makes jewels out of lumps of coal that have been tucked away deep in the earth,

14 Ibid., 90.
15 Lehnardt, Karen. *29 Brilliant Facts about the Sun,* https://www. factretriever.com/sun-facts, *November 30, 2016.*

waiting to be discovered. He flings out the flowers, rainbows, rivers, and sunsets and then invites you to join in the party. And what a celebration it is!

A number of years ago, I had the opportunity to live on the island of Kauai. It's the oldest island in the Hawaiian chain. While there, a friend of mine treated me to a one-hour ultralight ride that took me over the edge of the Waimea Canyon and along the shoreline of the Napali Coast. As the pilot and I slowly climbed up to 4,200 feet in the Australian-built ultralight with its multi-colored wing, I felt incredibly small as I looked out over the vast expanse of the canyon. Its colors captivated me. The black volcanic mountains were arrayed in the splendor of lush green foliage and brown and orange earth tones.

From there, we descended to the shores of the Napali Coast, buzzing beaches, and gliding through sugar cane fields. As I looked back over my shoulder, I was mesmerized by the volcanic cliffs along the coastline as they plummeted into the blue waters of the Pacific Ocean. The experience was both surreal and spiritual. On the one hand, I felt utterly insignificant among the immense surroundings of the canyon and ocean. But, on the other hand, I was also reminded that my heavenly Father has embraced me with His infinite love and I'm His special, one-of-a-kind boy!

Several years ago, I had the joy of returning to the beautiful island of Kauai with my family. Every day I went to the beach to indulge my senses in the breathtaking beauty of Hanalei Bay. I woke up each morning looking forward to the moment when I could breathe in the smell of the salt air and listen to the sounds and rhythms of the ocean. Its fragrances and "music" would always remind me of God, the extravagant Artist who, with utter abandon, loves to lavish us with *gifts*.

I loved playing on the beach with my grandchildren. Together, we were introduced to a world of wonder and creativity—driftwood became *swords*, as well as *tools* for building castles and roads. Holes in the surface of the sand were explored, only to reveal tiny *homes* for a variety of crabs. Even the waves of the ocean became *hurdles* over which to jump.

THE WONDERS OF THE DEEP

Someone once said that the *way* of God is in the sea. The ocean is one of the vast *theatres* in which God displays His extravagant creativity. For example, the oceans occupy nearly 71% of our planet's surface.[16] More than 97% of all our planet's water is contained in the ocean. The volume of water in our oceans, seas, and bays is estimated at 321,000,000 cubic miles.

The average depth of the ocean is approximately 12,200 feet. Its deepest point is 36,198 feet in the Mariana Trench in the western Pacific. Mount Everest, the highest point on the earth's surface, is a mile shorter than the deepest spot in the ocean. Water pressure, at the deepest point, is more than eight tons per square inch, the equivalent of one person trying to hold 50 jumbo jets.

Try to fathom this—an estimated 50-80% of all life on earth is found under the surface of the ocean. One swallow of seawater may contain millions of bacterial cells, hundreds of thousands of phytoplankton, and tens of thousands of zooplankton. Scientists have named and successfully classified 1.5 million species of life in the seas. But, it's estimated that there are between two million to 50 million more species still to be discovered.

The longest continuous mountain range known to exist in the Universe resides under the ocean at more than 40,000 miles long. The Great Barrier Reef, measuring 1,243 miles, is the largest "living" structure on Earth. It is so vast that it can actually be seen from the Moon. Its reefs are made up of 400 species of coral, supporting well over 2,000 different fish, 4,000 species of mollusk, and countless other invertebrates.

The blue whale is the largest animal on the planet and is bigger than the largest dinosaur. It can reach 110 feet in length and weigh more than 50 adult elephants. With a heart the size of a Volkswagen

---

16 Ocean facts taken from www.savethesea.org.

Beetle, the whale's blood vessels are so large that a full-grown trout can swim through them. To maintain its size, the blue whale has to consume up to four tons of krill a day.

Oceans are also a critical player in the air we breathe. Ocean plants produce half of the earth's oxygen. The waters of the ocean absorb nearly one-third of the human-caused carbon dioxide emissions. The seas also regulate the planet's temperatures. The oceans are truly a majestic display of God's infinite artistry!

Often, when I think about the ocean, I'm reminded of my first diving experience. It took place off the island of Maui, near a horseshoe-shaped rocky formation created by a once-active volcano. As I plunged into the dark depths 85 feet below the surface, I was introduced to an entirely different world that I had never experienced before. All my life, I had lived in cities or small towns. Although I had been intrigued by the ocean, I had never visited its depths. Yet, there I was, a bit wary about what I might encounter but excited about what I was to discover.

My first stop took me to a watery hole where a large moray eel nicknamed "Garbanzo" lived with his "girlfriend." From there, I was guided to a section of coral reef that housed a vast variety of life. I saw fish that looked like they were illumined by fluorescent lights, decked out in purple, red, and yellow colors. I watched as a shark eerily swam in the distance, gliding along effortlessly. I even found myself surrounded by small moray eels that were looking for a free meal.

But the highlight of the dive wasn't something that I saw, but something I *heard*. As I was swimming, taking in the mysterious surroundings that enveloped me, I heard an eerie sound in the distance that reminded me of a foghorn. I would later discover that what I had participated in was actually the music of migrating whales as they serenaded each other.

Some years later, I would find myself fascinated again by the wonders of the ocean. My wife and I were invited to travel and speak for thirteen weeks throughout Queensland, Australia. One of our scheduled stops took me to Mackay, a small city that, over the years, has grown along the edge of the enchanting Great Barrier Reef. The pastor who had invited us had planned a trip that would take us on a six-hour sailing excursion over the reef to a small cluster of islands where we would spend the night on the boat, anchored in a beautiful cove that looked like something out of a Hollywood movie.

As we glided through the waters in the 47-foot refurbished, wooden sailboat, I felt alive as I smelled the salt air and felt the rush of the wind and the spray of the ocean. Sea snakes escorted us along our journey as they surfaced from time to time to "catch their breath." That evening, one of the men who joined us on the trip *caught* our dinner, and then we were rocked to sleep by the gentle waves of the water.

I woke up the next morning determined to do some snorkeling before we set sail for our return trip to Mackay. What happened next would be a once-in-a-lifetime experience. As I was swimming and glancing into the beautiful waters of the cove, admiring the rock formations that plunged some 30 feet below to the ocean's floor, I soon realized that I had been joined by a school of large barracuda that swam effortlessly some 15 feet beneath me. God's gift to me that morning left an indelible imprint on my memory that I will never forget as long as I live.

EXTRAVAGANT LOVE

When we reflect on the immensity of the universe and all of the complexities of God's creativity, it's staggering to realize that we are the focus of His attention and the climax of creation. He made us for Himself and lavished His love upon us. We truly are a showcase of His infinite wisdom and handiwork—

> The human body is composed of nearly 100 trillion cells. Think of the skin—while water penetrates the skin outwardly, it cannot penetrate it inwardly. Think of the bones—capable of carrying a load thirty times greater than brick will support. Think of the liver—it breaks up old blood cells into bile and neutralizes poisonous substances. Think of the blood—ten to

twelve pints of a syrupy substance that distributes oxygen and carries away waste from tissues and organs, and also regulates the body's temperature. Think of the heart—weighing less than a pound, it's a real workhorse. On the average, it pumps 100,000 times every day, circulating 2000 gallons of blood through 60,000 miles of arteries, capillaries and veins.[17]

But we're not just tissue and bone, capillaries and veins. We've been made in the image of the One who made everything. And, He is fascinated by us! Brennan Manning said it best when he wrote,

> It is important to recapture the element of delight in creation. Imagine the ecstasy,…wonder, and delight when God makes a person in His own image—when God made you. The Father gave you as a gift to Himself. You are a response to the vast delight of God. Out of an infinite number of possibilities, God invested you with existence.[18]

Maybe you've never thought of yourself as a *gift* to the Father. Instead, you find yourself balking at the idea that you're special to Him. You probably think, "Why would the Creator of the universe even bother to think about me? I'm nothing. I have no talent. I really haven't done anything meaningful in my life. No one will even miss me when I die."

You may also feel this way because you're the one who rarely, if ever, gets invited out to eat. You're the one who goes unnoticed when you're in a crowd. No one asks your opinion about much of anything. And you find yourself spending countless hours all alone. So, it's only natural for you to assume that if people treat you this way, then God probably does as well.

If you could peer into the face of God, what kind of look do you think He would be giving you right now? Would His expression suggest that His patience is exhausted and He's fed up with

---

17 Nelson, Wilbur. *If I Were an Atheist* (Grand Rapids, MI: Baker, 1973), cited in *Our Daily Bread*, 6 August 1994.

18 Manning, Brennan. *Souvenirs of Solitude* (Colorado Springs, CO: NavPress, 2009), 143.

you? If you could hear Him say just one thing to you, would you hear the word "disappointed?"

If these are some of the personal issues that regularly haunt you, please let me remind you of what Jesus said in Matthew 10:29-31. He had *you* in mind when He spoke these words: "Are not two sparrows sold for a penny? Yet not one of them will fall to the ground apart from the will of your Father. So don't be afraid; you are worth more than many sparrows."

Sparrows certainly weren't any more valuable in Jesus' day than they are today.[19] In fact, sparrows were sometimes used for food by the poor. They were sold in pairs for a penny, which was approximately one-sixteenth of a man's average daily wage. Yet Jesus said that not *one* of them falls to the ground unnoticed by the Father.

Father cares about His sparrows! He gives them life and endows them with the ability to fly. He provides bugs and worms for them to feast on and places for them to nest. There are millions of sparrows in the world, yet Father knows each one.

It's intriguing to me that Jesus chose a simple sparrow to make His point about how valuable we are to Him. Out of approximately 9,000 species of birds, the Lord chose one of the most insignificant! Why? Because if Father is personally interested in a creature as unimpressive as the sparrow, how much more must He love and care for you? You are made in His image and redeemed by His Son. If Father takes the time to watch over the life of a tiny bird, how much more does He watch over you?

To drive home the point even more, Jesus went on to say that "even the very hairs of your head are all numbered" (v. 30). There are approximately 100,000 strands of hairs on the average head! You may have a bit more or quite a bit less, but God is keenly aware of all of them. He knows every little detail about you, and you are His delight!

---

19 Thoughts inspired from Sam Storms, *The Singing God* (Lake Mary, FL: Charisma House, 1998), 6.

In fact, when He thinks of you, He breaks out into endearing songs of affection. Does this sound too good to be true? Think again. Zephaniah 3:17 echoes these very sentiments:

> *The Lord your God is in the midst of you, a Mighty One, a Savior [Who saves]! He will rejoice over you with joy; He will rest [in silent satisfaction] and in His love He will be silent and make no mention [of past sins, or even recall them]; He will exult over you with singing* (AMP).

These words are stunning! While the language of this verse expresses God's exuberant love for Israel, it also richly conveys the depths of devotion and love that He feels for His children. If there ever was a verse worth dissecting and meditating on, it's verse 17. "The Lord your God is in the midst of you, a Mighty One, a Savior [Who saves]!" Just think of it. He is not only with you, but He is in you. He is right where you are, no matter where that may be. He has lovingly chosen to live with your smells, your hang-ups, your "highs" and your "lows," and He is extravagantly committed to you!

Notice, God will also "rejoice over you with joy." There's an uninhibited exuberance found in these words. Although some of you feel that you have failed Him far too many times for Him to rejoice over you, His love for you never changes. The issue isn't who you are or what you've done, but who He is. He's determined to *joyfully* love you, and that's all that matters!

As you continue your journey through Zephaniah 3:17, look closely at the words that come next in the text. "He will rest [in silent satisfaction] and in His love He will be silent and make no mention [of past sins, or even recall them]." Here we see a love so deeply felt that words are unnecessary.

Silence can often be the result of sheer contentment. I can remember times when I've sat in silence in a living room with my sons and just observed them. I have found myself absorbed in who they are, and just being with them has overcome me with feelings that simply can't be put into words. God is genuinely captivated by you! His silence, at times, is never a reflection of disinterest, but *enjoyment.* Palmer Robertson is correct: "To consider almighty God sinking in contemplations of love over a once-wretched human being can hardly be absorbed by the human mind."[20]

But if you think this is hard to absorb, return to Zephaniah 3:17 and notice the unmistakable language of the last phrase. It's the crowning jewel of the verse. It passionately proclaims that God "will exult over you with singing." God loves you with such fervency that He leaps for joy, dances, and celebrates your life with singing!

Earlier we discovered that God's love for us often reduces Him to silent adoration. Yet, He eventually has to shatter the silence with songs of delight! The One who sang the first solo and gave birth to sounds and rhythms can't hold back His feelings for us! We're His sons and daughters; we're the "apple of His eye." And, He's *happy* that we belong to Him!

Singing enables the heart to express deeply felt emotions that mere speaking can't communicate. Singing can do things that words alone can't accomplish. This is why Father wants us to know that His love for us is so extravagant that He can't help but sing over us!

However, there are some theologians who strongly insist that God doesn't have these kinds of passions and emotions. They're concerned about God appearing weak or subject to "fickle feelings." While we need to be sensitive to their concerns, we dare not limit the words of Zephaniah 3:17 to mere figures of speech. Although we can't fully comprehend the nature and character of God, the Scriptures clearly indicate that He feels—He has emotions, passions, and powerful affections for each of us!

This is nowhere more vividly portrayed than in the parable of the prodigal son or, as it should be called, the story of the *extravagant* Father. We find it recorded in Luke 15:11-32:

---

20 Robertson, O. Palmer. *The Books of Nahum, Habakkuk, and Zephaniah* (Grand Rapids, MI: Eerdmans, 1990), 340.

There was once a man who had two sons. The younger said to his father, 'Father, I want right now what's coming to me.'

So the father divided the property between them. It wasn't long before the younger son packed his bags and left for a distant country. There, undisciplined and dissipated, he wasted everything he had. After he had gone through all his money, there was a bad famine all through that country and he began to hurt. He signed on with a citizen there who assigned him to his fields to slop the pigs. He was so hungry he would have eaten the corncobs in the pig slop, but no one would give him any.

That brought him to his senses. He said, 'All those farm-hands working for my father sit down to three meals a day, and here I am starving to death. I'm going back to my father. I'll say to him, Father, I've sinned against God, I've sinned before you; I don't deserve to be called your son. Take me on as a hired hand.' He got right up and went home to his father.

When he was still a long way off, his father saw him. His heart pounding, he ran out, embraced him, and kissed him. The son started his speech: 'Father, I've sinned against God, I've sinned before you; I don't deserve to be called you son ever again.'

But the father wasn't listening. He was calling to the servants, 'Quick. Bring a clean set of clothes and dress him. Put the family ring on his finger and sandals on his feet. Then get a grain-fed heifer and roast it. We're going to feast! We're going to have a wonderful time! My son is here—given up for dead and now alive! Given up for lost and now found!' And they began to have a wonderful time.

All this time his older son was out in the field. When the day's work was done he came in. As he approached the house, he heard the music and dancing. Calling over one of the houseboys, he asked what was going on. He told him,

*'Your brother came home. Your father has ordered a feast—
barbecued beef!—because he has him home safe and sound.'*

*The older brother stalked off in an angry sulk and re-
fused to join in. His father came out and tried to talk to him,
but he wouldn't listen. The son said, 'Look how many years
I've stayed here serving you, never giving you one moment
of grief, but have you ever thrown a party for me and my
friends? Then this son of yours who has thrown away your
money on whores shows up and you go all out with a feast!'*

*His father said, 'Son, you don't understand. You're with
me all the time, and everything that is mine is yours—but
this is a wonderful time, and we had to celebrate. This brother of yours was dead, and he's alive! He was lost, and he's
found!'* (TM).

This parable is really a portrait of our heavenly Father and
what He's actually like. There's probably not a more passionate,
picturesque statement about Him in the entire Bible than what is
conveyed in verse 20: When the father saw his wayward son, he
"...ran to his son, threw his arms around him and kissed him."

Instead of portraying God as a bookkeeping, divine legalist,
Jesus introduces us to a *father* who dances for sheer joy at the sight
of a devastated son who is returning home. He depicts the *father*
as a divine sprinter, who runs after outcasts and throws parties for
those who can't possibly qualify for His favor. Even "wayward"
children are the objects of His intense longings and affections.

Have you met this *father*? He wants to dance into your life
and celebrate what His grace has accomplished for you. He wants
to draw you into His heart and embrace you with His love. Furthermore, He wants to lead you into all that He has destined for
you to be!

Someone once wrote,

When I meditated on the word Guidance, I kept seeing
"dance" at the end of the word. I remember reading that doing
God's will is a lot like dancing. When two people try to lead,

nothing feels right. The movement doesn't flow with the music, and everything is quite uncomfortable and jerky. When one person realizes that, and lets the other lead, both bodies begin to flow with the music. One gives gentle cues, perhaps with a nudge to the back or by pressing lightly in one direction or another. It's as if two become one body, moving beautifully. The dance takes surrender, willingness, and attentiveness from one person and gentle guidance and skill from the other.

My eyes drew back to the word Guidance. When I saw "G" I thought of God, followed by "u" and "i." "God," "u" and "i" dance. God you and I dance.[21]

In a universe of wonder and extravagant creativity, faith is not a desperate search for what is "predictable." It's holding on tightly while God leads us in a dance and shows us one *improbable* step after another. Faith is nothing less than dancing with childlike abandon on the dance floor of God's world!

I danced in the morning when the world was begun,
And I danced in the moon and the stars and the sun,
And I came down from Heaven and I danced on the earth.
At Bethlehem I had my birth.

I danced for the scribe and the Pharisee,
But they would not dance and they would not follow me,
I danced for the fishermen, for James and John;
They came to me and the Dance went on.

"Dance, then, wherever you may be;
I am the Lord of the Dance," said he,
"And I'll lead you all wherever you may be,
And I'll lead you all in the Dance," said he.[22]

---

21 Source Unknown
22 Words: Sydney Carter
   Copyright © 1963 Stainer & Bell, Ltd. (Admin. Hope Publishing Company, Carol Stream, IL 60188). All rights reserved. Used by permission.

4   BREATHTAKING BEAUTY

Beauty has the capacity to stir the soul in a way very few things can. It calls to us, fascinates us, and overwhelms us. While we can't necessarily explain why something is beautiful, we are inherently drawn to it. It always compels a response from us because it touches something deep within our hearts.

Beauty is what amazes us and takes our breath away. It arouses passions and emotions that can't easily be articulated. It causes our hearts to beat faster and sends chills up and down our spines. Beauty can be encountered in the glowing colors of a lingering sunset, the vast expanse of a canyon, or the birth of a baby. It can be seen in a landscape, a painting, or in a garden of flowers. It can be heard in the melody, harmony, and rhythm of a song. It can be experienced in the scent of a flower or the fragrance of perfume. It can even be *clothed* in compassion, *modeled* through moral excellence, or *treasured* in the triumph of truth and justice.

Because we've been made in the image of God, we have the capacity to acknowledge and appreciate beauty in all of its forms. We even share in the *divine ability* to both create and celebrate it. But, whatever beauty we see and experience in this life is just a dim reflection of a *breathtaking beauty* that is "out of this world." It calls to us every moment of our lives. It arouses a longing deep within our hearts for intimacy. It fuels our search for meaning and wholeness. It evokes a yearning for something more than the world can offer. And, this *beauty* that calls to us is none other than God Himself!

DIVINE BEAUTY

The *beauty of God* has intrigued me for years. I have found my-self fascinated by the mystery that surrounds it. Yet what saddens me is the fact that many theological books have omitted the subject of *divine beauty* altogether. God's beauty has even been left out of the traditional list of His attributes. But, as Augustine discovered, God is beauty itself. He spoke of Him as "my Father, supremely good, beauty of all things beautiful."[23] While all of us would con-cede that God is the source of all beauty, how many of us would actually be comfortable with what Augustine meant?

What is *divine beauty*? The beauty of God is that *quality* about Him which makes Him supremely attractive and desirable. It's what should leave us in *awe* of His divine perfections. Like a rare and exquisite diamond, the beauty of God has many facets. His *per-sonality* is rich, deep, and infinitely appealing. There is something about Him that is more pleasing and fulfilling than anything life has to offer.

> Divine beauty is so vastly superior to the very best of created splendors that we cannot come close to conceiving it. This is true of every divine perfection. God is not only the fullness of joy. He is the very essence of joy, purest ecstasy, delight without limit.... So also he is purest loveliness, purest wisdom, purest love, all with no end whatever.[24]

The psalmists spoke of the beauty of God as *glory*, an incom-parable splendor that transcends anything imaginable. "The glory of the Lord, therefore, is the supereminently luminous beauty of divinity beyond all experience and all descriptions, all categories, a beauty before which all earthly splendors, marvelous as they are, pale into insignificance."[25]

---

23 *The Confessions of St. Augustine*, translated with an introduction and notes by John K. Ryan (New York: Image Books, 1960), 3, 6.
24 Dubay, Thomas. *The Evidential Power of Beauty* (San Francisco, CA: Ignatius Press, 1999), 296.
25 Ibid., 45.

While God's beauty is revealed in creation, as well as Scripture, it's *perfectly reflected* in the face of Christ. Everything about Jesus is beautiful—His life, His ministry, and even His death! In the Incarnation, the *Word* became flesh. The *radiant representation* of the Godhead became human. The Son of God became one of us! This is the *wonder* of the birth of Christ!

In the Incarnation, Jesus made beautiful all that it means to be "truly" human. In his book, *Redeeming Beauty*, theologian Aidan Nichols reinforces this truth: "The Incarnation is the divine means of transfiguring the world into greater beauty precisely by redeeming the divine image in man from the deformity of sin...."[26]

> In the Incarnation and redemption divinity is shown best of all in the emptying of the Son in taking on our human nature and in the atrocity of his Passion and death on the Cross....The beauty here is the unspeakable love of the Father and the Son for ungrateful sinners....Far, far beyond all created beauties...is the divine glory that shines out from this unsurpassable love found in the torture of Holy Week: Perfection himself whipped to blood, crowned with thorns, mocked, spit upon, ridiculed, nailed, pierced—all because he loves you and me, who have in return sinned against him. In this consummate ugliness, this unspeakable outrage shines a picture of divine beauty immeasurably beyond all earthly splendors; utter love from the depths of kenosis, the divine emptying....[27]

RESPONDING TO BEAUTY

To live in the reality of God's beauty is truly why we exist. Yet so many today are unaware of this truth. If you would press them to explain the purpose for their existence, they would probably suggest that God gave them life so they could glorify Him in what they do. But, for many of these same individuals, "glorifying God"

---

26 Nichols, Aidan. *Redeeming Beauty* (London, UK: Ashgate Publishing Company, 2007), 78.

27 Dubay, Thomas. *The Evidential Power of Beauty* (San Francisco, CA: Ignatius Press, 1999), 310-311.

is an empty phrase. Ask them to describe what it means or how it's done, and you're likely to get a blank stare.

While *glorifying God* has become somewhat of a cliché in evangelical circles, many of us have never been challenged to think about what a life that glorifies God is supposed to look like. So, what does it look like, and how can our lives ultimately glorify Him?

To help answer these questions, we need to return to a statement in the Westminster Catechism that I mentioned in a previous chapter. Seventeenth-century theologians, contemplating the reason for man's existence, concluded that "the chief end of man is to glorify God and to enjoy Him forever." But were these men talking about two distinct things—glorifying God and enjoying Him? Or, were they clearly implying something else?

It has been suggested that the best way to capture the real meaning of what was written by these theologians is to replace the word "and" with "by." Notice carefully how the statement now reads: "The chief end of man is to glorify God *by* enjoying Him forever."[28] Could it be that the best way to honor God in our lives and celebrate His goodness is to rejoice in the revelation of who He is and to bask in His beauty? Is it possible that God is glorified in us the most when our knowledge and experience of Him so captivate our hearts that He becomes the supreme joy and passion of our lives?

Jonathan Edwards, in a sermon entitled *Nothing upon Earth Can Represent the Glories of Heaven*, sheds some light on this issue for us. Edwards said that "God created man for nothing else but happiness. He created him only that He might communicate happiness to him."[29] But how could God have created us for *happiness*

---

28 Piper, John. *Desiring God* (Sisters, OR: Multnomah Publishers Inc., 1996), 17-18.
29 Edwards, Jonathan. *Sermons and Discourses 1723-1729*, The Works of Jonathan Edwards, Volume 14. Edited by Kenneth P. Minkema (New Haven: Yale University Press, 1997), 145-146.

if He really created us for His *glory*? These two concepts appear to contradict each other.

However, these seemingly incompatible ideas are *not* at odds with each other at all. God is truly glorified in us when we are delighting in Him! We were born to experience His breathtaking beauty and find our ultimate happiness in Him!

Enjoying God is not a secondary issue in the Christian life; it's not even a means to an end. It is the end! The purpose of our existence is the pursuit of our enjoyment in God. It's discovering a joy that transcends disappointment and heartache; it's savoring a satisfaction that surpasses abundance or adversity. The happiness for which we were created is found in celebrating the fact that such a beautiful and wonderful God is ours! The Psalmist David seemed to grasp the grandeur of this extraordinary truth in a way few individuals ever have. He even went so far as to passionately express his feelings in Psalm 27:4: "One thing I ask of the LORD, this is what I seek: that I may dwell in the house of the LORD all the days of my life, to gaze upon the beauty of the LORD, and to seek him in His temple."

In light of David's responsibilities as King of Israel and the pressing issues he continually faced, his identity could have easily been absorbed in his calling as the king of God's people. But his resolve was remarkable. He chose to find his identity in God's extravagant affections for him. When David could have looked elsewhere for comfort and relief, he found solace in the delightful, incomparable, awe-inspiring beauty of the One who loved him! David could've had anything his heart desired; but God was the *primary* object of his pursuit throughout life. David couldn't get enough of the Lord! He yearned for just *one thing*—to encounter God in His uncreated beauty. David wanted to experience everything he could of what makes God so attractive and desirable.

Thomas Dubay once wrote that *wonder* is the normal response to splendor. While we have already seen this graphically illustrated in David's experience with God, we can see this even more vividly portrayed in Isaiah 6:1-3. The veil is pulled back on eternity, and we come upon a scene that is both majestic and mysterious. Six-winged creatures, hovering around the throne of God, are heard crying, "'Holy, holy, holy, is the LORD Almighty; the whole earth is full of his glory'" (v. 3).

As we reflect on this "eternal moment," we may find ourselves a bit intrigued by the response of the seraphim to the splendor of the Lord. Are they crying out of intimidation and fear? Are they engaged in mechanical obedience to some heavenly liturgy? Or, are these six-winged creatures actually encountering aspects of God's unique personality (holiness) in such an intense, invigorating way that all they can do is respond this way? Imagine these creatures experiencing the *undiluted, overpowering pleasure* of His beauty to such a degree that they have to cover their faces. For them, it's never about fear or duty; it's always about fascination and delight.

Why do the seraphim never cease to adore the beautiful God who made them? Is there someone more splendid? Is there another more breathtakingly beautiful? What else could possibly compare to the joy and delight of being loved by the holy One? What could rival such experiences?

The scene depicted in Isaiah 6 is a vivid illustration of what David was trying to portray in Psalm 29:2—a worship born out of the "beauty of holiness" (NKJV). Wonder and worship are the normal responses to splendor. God's holiness is His beauty revealed! It's who He is. It's what makes Him unique and distinct from all others. God is in a "league" all by Himself; yet, He delights in sharing Himself with His creation.

But what's disturbing is that *holiness* has often been equated with religious rules and regulations, dress codes, and "personal convictions" imposed on others by the *spiritually elite*. As a result, *holiness* has appeared to a lot of us as unattractive and undesirable. God's holiness has even been seen as nothing more than that quality in Him that abhors sin. While God has always been deeply grieved by the consequences of sin, He chose to identify with outcasts and enter their world so they could identify with Him and enter His world. And, it's the experience of His beauty and worth that will truly bring freedom and joy to each of our lives!

TRANSFORMED BY BEAUTY

The encounter of the human heart with the beauty of God is truly liberating and enjoyable. But, it's also profoundly *transforming*! I believe this is what Paul was referring to in 2 Corinthians 3:18 when he wrote, "But we all, with unveiled face, beholding as in a mirror the glory of the Lord, are being transformed into the same image from glory to glory, just as by the Spirit of the Lord" (NKJV).

Encountering the beauty of the Lord will reshape our lives and capture our hearts. It will expose the *ugliness* of the consequences of sin and the futility of giving ourselves to the deceptively attractive facades of temptation. It will evoke love in us and create new affections that no power can overcome. And, it will produce a joy and happiness in us with which nothing can compare!

All of us pursue some measure of happiness, whether we want to admit it or not. But the real issue is to *whom* or to *what* will we turn in order to find it? So many people today are desperate for anything that will bring excitement or pleasure to their otherwise boring existence. They're usually willing to pay whatever price it takes in order to get it, regardless of the consequences.

But human happiness will never *ultimately* be found in a six-figure income, illicit sexual gratification, the euphoria or exhilaration of drugs, or in any earthly pleasure or achievement. While some things may *not* be wrong in themselves, nothing can give us the satisfaction we crave outside of experiencing the beauty and pleasure of the One who made us.

Enjoying God will bring a fulfillment to our lives that no human pleasure can rival. It offers us the ultimate solution for our struggles, and it gives us the power to embrace a love-empowered life. Finding our happiness in God is truly the catalyst for living as His sons and daughters!

All too often, we have viewed the Christian life as consisting of rules and restrictions that attempt to suppress our desire for happiness and deprive us of the pleasures of life. But nothing could be farther from the truth. God has never denied us anything that is beneficial to our *ultimate* satisfaction and happiness. He has only warned us of those unhealthy pleasures that will lead to our misery, shame, and regret.

Sin is the misguided pursuit of happiness and pleasure in places where only emptiness and disappointment are found. Sin is turning down God's offer of the pleasure of His presence for the wrong kinds of things that will never fully satisfy the longings of our hearts. Or, as C. S. Lewis once wrote:

> We are half-hearted creatures, fooling about with drink and sex and ambition when infinite joy is offered us, like an ignorant child who wants to go on making mud pies in a slum because he cannot imagine what is meant by the offer of a holiday at the sea. We are far too easily pleased.[30]

When Paul, in 2 Timothy 3:4, warned about those who would become lovers of pleasure rather than lovers of God, he was writing to individuals who would pursue pleasure *without* God. The key words in this verse are "rather than," and they highlight the stark contrast between the people who seek a sensual, self-indulgent pleasure that is *God-less* and those who seek their satisfaction in the pleasure of God's love.

God is the all-satisfying One who made us for Himself. He invites us to indulge ourselves in all that He has provided in Christ, and He longs to lavish His beauty and goodness on each of us. Remember, God's greatest glory is demonstrated in our ultimate delight in Him. Therefore, the primary goal of our lives should be the pursuit of pleasure in Him!

When Jesus calls us to deny ourselves and follow Him (Mark 8:34-37), He's actually encouraging us to pursue our ultimate happiness and pleasure. While this may be hard for some of us to

30 Lewis, C. S. *The Weight of Glory and Other Addresses* (New York: Touchstone, 1996), 25-26.

believe, Jesus never intends for us to view the "denial of self" as an end in itself. He is inviting us to deny ourselves the *counterfeit* pleasures of this life in order to gain the unending pleasures of being loved by Him.

For us to not follow Jesus is to *deny ourselves* the greatest joy imaginable! His call to us is to reject any attempt to satisfy the longings of our hearts through any illegitimate pleasure. Instead, His invitation to us is to follow Him and gain true life, true joy, and true pleasure!

All too often, preachers have challenged believers to deny themselves the unhealthy, phony pleasures of this life while making the mistake of not introducing their listeners to the incomparable worth and beauty of God. Rather than being motivated by the supreme satisfaction that comes from being loved by Him, many Christians have subsequently tried to *deny self* out of fear or condemnation. But a "denying of self" that is not based on the greater goal of experiencing and enjoying the beauty of the Lord will inevitably lead to legalism and religious pride. It's only the unfolding discovery of the value of Jesus that truly enables an individual to live free and fulfilled!

In Matthew 13:44, Jesus introduced to His hearers a parable about the kingdom of God. He said, "Again, the kingdom of heaven is like treasure hidden in a field, which a man found and hid; and for joy over it he goes and sells all that he has and buys that field" (NKJV). Notice the phrase "and for joy over it." It was the *joy* of discovering the treasure that motivated the man to sell everything he had.

To better appreciate the scope of this parable, I believe we need to look at this verse from two different angles. First of all, it's highly likely that the "man" referred to in this parable was none other than Jesus Himself, and the treasure that prompted Him to sell everything He owned was the lives of men and women of all generations.

In turn, when we begin to grasp the Lord's passion for us and we see ourselves as His joy and treasure, we will be motivated to joyfully and extravagantly give ourselves completely to our *Treasure*.

Commenting on Jesus' parable in Matthew 13:44, Joachim Jeremias wrote:

> When that great joy surpassing all measure seizes a man, it carries him away, penetrates his inmost being, subjugates his mind. All else seems valueless compared to that surpassing worth. No price is too great to pay. The unreserved surrender of what is most valuable becomes a matter of course. The decisive thing in the parable is not what the man gives up, but his reason for doing so—the overwhelming experience of their discovery.... The effect of the joyful news is overpowering; it fills the heart with gladness...[31]

The Apostle Paul wrote in Romans 3:23 that "...all have sinned and fall short of the glory of God." But what did he mean by "falling short" of God's glory? The clearest answer to this question is found in Romans 1:21-23:

> For although they knew God, they neither glorified him as God, nor gave thanks to him, but their thinking became futile and their foolish hearts were darkened. Although they claimed to be wise, they became fools and exchanged the glory of the immortal God for images made to look like mortal man and birds and animals and reptiles.

The way anyone "falls short" of God's glory (beauty, goodness) is to exchange it for something that's inferior and of lesser value. "All sin stems from failing to place supreme value on the glory and goodness of God. We exchange a priceless treasure for the trinkets of this world."[32] We believe the lie of temptation which suggests that sin will make us happier than God ever could. But, in reality, sin is not the gaining of pleasure but, rather, the loss of pleasure!

31 Jeremias, Joachim. *The Parables of Jesus* (New York: Charles Scribner and Sons, 1970), 84.

32 Hill, S. J. *Enjoying God* (Lake Mary, FL: Passio, Charisma Media/ Charisma House Book Group, 2012), 131.

Sin isn't just turning our backs on the beauty of who God is; sin is really turning our backs on *life*. Think about it—so much of our frustration, misery, and shame in life have been the result of giving our hearts to *counterfeit joys*.

So, why do we continue to hold on to the very things that continue to bring us so much pain and disillusionment? Maybe we believe the lies of temptation because we have been so blinded to the beauty of God that He often doesn't appear as attractive to us as sin. As a result, fornication and adultery seem to be a lot more appealing than being intimate with Jesus; getting "stoned" sounds far more exciting than being filled with the Spirit; and living a self-absorbed, self-indulgent life appears to be a lot more fun than loving the poor and needy.

Maybe we cling to old habits because we think we deserve them. We remind ourselves of all the things we've had to endure and the many times people have let us down, and we retreat into the arms of our "counterfeit lovers." Or, we believe God has disappointed us so much that we allow ourselves the right to indulge in the pleasures of sin.

Maybe we hold on to *counterfeit joys* because we can't imagine living without them. We convince ourselves that we can't face our boredom apart from them. We think that the only way we can cope with our loneliness and rejection is to try to deaden the pain with things that will bring us some measure of comfort.

But, when all is said and done, we continue to cling to our *counterfeit joys* because our *inferior pleasures* are enjoyable. Regardless of how temporary they may be, they are still *joys*. We constantly revert to them because they work, at least for the moment. This is why we have to replace our *lesser joys* with a more "pleasing" joy—a joy that satisfies forever, not just for the moment. We have to discover a pleasure that never ends (Psalm 16:11). We have to embrace the promise of superior happiness that can only be found in our Father's unending love!

But what do we do when temptation is staring us in the face? How do we respond when sin is enticing us, appearing so attractive and alluring? The answers to these questions are actually found in a mythical legend about a mysterious island, two brave warriors, and some very "beautiful women."[33]

According to the story, Paris, the prince of Troy, had kidnapped the wife of Menelaus, the King of Greece. Menelaus, along with Ulysses and a mighty Greek army, set out to rescue Helen and restore dignity to their beloved country.

Hidden in the belly of a huge wooden horse, Ulysses and his men gained access to the city in which Paris had fled. They slaughtered its inhabitants and rescued Helen, the woman "whose face launched a thousand ships." But their return voyage home would prove to be even more challenging.

While much has been written about Ulysses' encounter with the witch Circe and his heroic exploits in blinding the Cyclops Polyphemus, what may be the most intriguing aspect of this adventure is the legend of the mysterious island inhabited by Sirens (demonic creatures impersonating beautiful women). Countless sailors, passing by this island, had succumbed to the outward beauty of the Sirens and their seductive songs. Once these men had been lured close to shore, their boats had crashed on the rocks hidden beneath the surface of the water. According to the myth, the Sirens had drawn the sailors to land, had proceeded to kill every one of them, and had savagely eaten their flesh.

Ulysses had frequently been warned about the Sirens and their seductive songs. Upon reaching the intriguing island, he ordered his sailors to put wax in their ears so they wouldn't be drawn to their destruction. He commanded them not to look to the left or right but to row for their very lives. But Ulysses had different plans for himself. He instructed his men to tie him to the mast of the ship with his ears unplugged. "I want to hear their song. No matter what I say or do, don't untie me until we are safely at a distance from the island."

---

33 The section dealing with the legend of Ulysses and Jason was inspired by a story written by Sam Storms in *Pleasures Evermore* (Colorado Springs, CO: NavPress Publishing Group, 2000), 104-106.

Still, the songs of the Sirens were more than Ulysses could resist. Even though he knew better, he let himself become seduced by their sound and the promise of immediate sexual gratification. One Siren even took on the form of his wife, Penelope, hoping to allure him to shore. Were it not for the ropes that held him tightly to the mast of the ship, Ulysses would have succumbed to their beauty. Although his arms and hands were restrained, his heart was captivated by their seductive ways.

Ulysses' strategy for resisting the Sirens appears very similar to the way many believers attempt to live the Christian life. Although they know what's at stake, they struggle through life saying "no" to sin because their arms and hands have been restrained by the laws and prohibitions imposed upon them by their religious environment. Their obedience is nothing more than a reluctant conformity to rules and regulations born out of fear and shame.

SURRENDERING TO A SUPERIOR SOUND

Jason, like Ulysses, was also a character of ancient Greek mythology. He was probably best known for his pursuit of the famous Golden Fleece. Like Ulysses, he encountered the seductive sounds of the Sirens. But Jason's strategy for facing the torrid temptation would be completely different from that of Ulysses'.

Jason brought with him on the perilous journey a man named Orpheus. Orpheus was a highly skilled musician who excelled on the flute and lyre. When his music was played it had a captivating effect on all who heard it. His melodies and sounds were unequaled in the entire ancient world.

When it came time for Jason and his crew to sail past the mysterious island, Jason decided not to plug the ears of his men. Neither did he instruct his sailors to tie him to the mast of the ship to restrain any lustful urge that he may have. Even though he was no less determined than Ulysses to resist the enticement of the Sirens, he, instead, chose a different solution.

Jason ordered Orpheus to play his most beautiful songs. The captivating sounds of the flute and lyre overpowered the seductive sounds of the Sirens. Jason and his men were able to resist the melodies coming from the island because they heard a more sublime sound. They experienced something that was far superior to what was being offered them. They tasted something that was far sweeter than the sexy ways of the Sirens.

While both Jason and Ulysses survived the ordeal, only Jason was changed by it. Neither man had succumbed to the temptation, but only one had truly overcome! Jason believed that the captivating effect of a superior sound would not only empower him to triumph over temptation, but it would enable him to experience a more satisfying joy.

How many of us, like Ulysses, are in survival mode when it comes to temptation and sin? We know what we should do, but we continue to fight against the restrictive ropes of religious rules. We wrestle with the binding power of shame and the fear of punishment, while our hearts still yearn for what is taboo! No wonder we experience very little change.

How many of us are bound by lust, burdened with shame, battling with bitterness, or bored stiff? We know that Jesus promised us an "abundant life" (John 10:10), and Peter talked about a "joy inexpressible and full of glory" (1 Peter 1:8). Yet, we look at our lives and things just don't add up. A number of us have even read various "how to" books, sought counseling, and followed carefully laid out programs. But, we still feel hopeless and disillusioned.

The problem is that we have tried to motivate ourselves to *obey* by reminding ourselves of the consequences of our choices or what it might feel like if we ever get caught. We've even attempted to convince ourselves of the ugliness and futility of sin. However, the only way to become free from the slavery of sin is to cultivate a superior passion for enjoying the beauty of who God is.

But what does it mean to experience the beauty of God, and how can we practically enjoy Him? While I'm going to be addressing these questions in a later chapter entitled, *Beholding God*, I want to highlight something that continues to make an impact on my life. If we're ever going to cultivate a passion for living in the beauty of God, we will have to remind ourselves continually that we are enveloped in our Father's perfect love every minute of the day. He is closer to us than the air we breathe. The more we're aware of His presence in and around us, the easier it will be to encounter Him and enjoy Him in very tangible ways.

All too often, we have allowed the failures of the past or the fears of the future to determine our focus. This has kept us from seeing the beauty of God that surrounds us every second of the day. We have failed to understand that what we focus on will always dictate what we experience in any given moment. Being absorbed in the past or future will always cause us to miss the *wonder* of the present.

Whether we realize it or not, the way we presently view the world around us was primarily chosen for us, not by us. We inherited a way of looking at the world that was passed on to us by our parents, friends, media, and society in general. While our personal life's experiences have also played a major role in the way our minds have been *programmed*, outside factors have been "wiring" our brains from almost the moment we were born.

Although some of the ways we have been *wired* to view life have been beneficial, many of them have also been very detrimental. Much of our thinking has involved viewing and experiencing life as if God was *not* present with us. The only way to change this is to become more single-minded, submitting ourselves to Him in the present moment. Regardless of what is going on around us, we must try to remain aware of His loving presence.

When you notice that your thoughts have drifted away from God, don't get frustrated or upset with yourself. Simply remind yourself that the only thing that matters is the present moment. Reflect on His immeasurable love and affection for you displayed in His life and death. Think about aspects of His personality that you've discovered in this book that may have intrigued you. Or, stop and take a deep breath and let yourself take in your surroundings. You'll discover that you can observe God's beauty in the face of a stranger or the smile of a friend. You can experience His beauty in the cooing of a baby or in the cloud formations overhead. You can even encounter the Lord's beauty in the fragrance of a flower, the leaves of a tree, or the sounds of a bird.

Let your heart come alive to all the wonderful gifts with which Father has surrounded you. Capture the moment and let His embrace invigorate you. Enjoy your life! And always remember—

> When you become a Christian, when you decide to follow Christ, you decide in favor of passion. Jesus came to forgive us of our sin, yes, but His mission was also to introduce us to the passion of living. Most people believe that following Jesus is all about living right. Not true. Following Jesus is all about living fully.[34]

---

34 Yaconelli, Michael. *Dangerous Wonder* (Colorado Springs, CO: NavPress Publishing Group, 1998), 94.

"It's truly godlike to be humble as it is to be exalted."[35] So wrote Colin E. Gunton in his book, *The Christian Faith: An Introduction to Christian Doctrine*. Such language sounds very similar to the words of the Apostle Paul in 1 Corinthians 1:25: "...the *weakness* of God is stronger than man's strength" (italics added). As you reflect on these two statements, what are your first impressions? Let me guess. You may be having a hard time wrapping your mind around the language. You may even be asking yourself, "How can the qualities of *humility* and *weakness* ever be attributed to an all-powerful God?"

Yet there is an "inner part" of God that has often been hidden behind His brilliant splendor and all-encompassing power. It's also a part of Him that has been misunderstood since the beginning of time. It stands out in stark contrast to the wisdom and might of man. This "inner part" of God is His willingness and desire to demonstrate His power and greatness through *humility* and *weakness*. As you're about to discover, this pattern is woven throughout the pages of Scripture.

DELIVERED BY A LAMB

Lambs are such gentle-looking creatures, with their spindly legs and soft wool. They appear to be the very symbol of vulnerability. Maybe this is why we always want to protect them. But in the wisdom of God, a *lamb* was actually used to liberate His people from the tyranny of Pharaoh.

---

35 Gunton, Colin E. *The Christian Faith: An Introduction to Christian Doctrine* (Oxford: Blackwell, 2002), 181.

Abraham's descendants had been living in northern Egypt for 400 years (Genesis 15:13). They had grown in number to several million people. Pharaoh felt threatened, so he made slaves of them and subjected them to inhumane conditions. In their utter desperation, they cried out to the Lord for help. Because of the covenant promises He had made to Abraham, God chose a man by the name of Moses to lead the Hebrew people out of slavery.

Pharaoh was given every conceivable chance to let the Hebrew slaves go free, but he refused. His arrogance opened the door for terrible demonic plagues to be unleashed against his nation. But just prior to the *destroyer* killing all the firstborn of Egypt (Exodus 12:23), God gave Moses detailed instructions that would protect His people from the plague of death.

The Lord said to Moses, "'This month is to be for you the first month, the first month of your year'" (Exodus 12:2). God was clearly indicating that He was about to do something for His people that would be like the first month of the rest of their lives. They were about to experience a new beginning under His loving guidance and care.

This new beginning would start with the consumption of a "lamb." God further said to Moses, "'Tell the whole community of Israel that on the tenth day of this month each man is to take a lamb for his family, one for each household'" (Exodus 12:3). Every man was to choose a lamb without blemish for his family. He was to select it on the tenth day of the month, and then he was to observe the lamb until the fourteenth day to make sure there was nothing wrong with it.

On the fourteenth day of the month, every man was to bring his lamb to the doorstep of his home and kill it. As he killed the animal, he was instructed to catch the blood in a basin. Then he was to take a hyssop bush, dip it in the blood, and sprinkle the blood above and on both sides of the doorpost. As a result, the entire entrance into the house would be covered with blood.

Since the Hebrew day began at six o'clock in the evening, the men had to kill the lambs around three o'clock in the afternoon in order to eat the meal by six o'clock. So when three o'clock arrived, the lambs were killed and the blood was applied to the doorposts. Every family then entered their home through the bloodstained door. Once inside, they roasted the lamb and ate it as they waited for the plague of death to move through the land of Egypt. Since the lamb had to be totally consumed, small families were asked to join with their neighbors so they, together, could eat the entire lamb (Exodus 12:4).

As the scent of the cooked lambs ascended into heaven, God was reminded of the covenant He had made with Abraham and the ram He had provided for a sacrifice. The smell of the smoke was further evidence to the Lord that the blood of the covenant had been applied on behalf of Abraham's descendants. The families that sprinkled the blood of the lamb on their doorposts would be saved from the *destroyer*.

The Lord also told His people, "'Do not leave any of it (the lamb) till morning; if some is left till morning, you must burn it. This is how you are to eat it; with your cloak tucked into your belt, your sandals on your feet and your staff in your hand. Eat it in haste; it is the Lord's Passover'" (Exodus 12:10-11, emphasis added).

With every person having feasted on a lamb, the Hebrew people were ready to take their journey to freedom. As they marched out of Egypt, a lamb was in each of them. God delivered His people, not with a mighty army, but through the death of a *lamb*.

THE POWER OF A CRIPPLED ARMY

After Israel had crossed the Red Sea, they wandered in the desert for 40 years. They failed to enter the Land of Canaan because of their unbelief and hardness of heart. So God raised up a new generation to embrace what He had promised them. But before they could take possession of their inheritance, the men were given specific instructions in preparation for the conquering of Canaan.

This new generation of men had not been circumcised, and they still carried the "reproach of Egypt" with them. The very memory of Israel's enslavement in Egypt had to be removed. So what were the Lord's instructions concerning the men who were planning to go into battle against their enemies? Did He have them circumcised on the eastern banks of the Jordan River where they would have sufficient time to recover before they attacked the Canaanites? If that had happened, the Israelites at least would've had the added protection of high waters, because the Jordan was flooding her banks at that time of the year.

Instead, God led His people across the Jordan River and watched as the sons of Israel were circumcised and "crippled" right under the noses of the mighty men of Jericho. The Lord allowed them to be *weakened* in the presence of their enemies! The people must've been terrified as they watched their young men incapacitated by the stroke of a knife. But at the very time God's army was being *weakened*, the hearts of the enemies of Israel *melted* and "... they no longer had the courage to face the Israelites" (Joshua 5:1). It was the obedience of God's people and their identification with the Lord's *way* of weakness that brought fear to their enemies!

GIDEON'S WEAKENED 300

Victory, God's way, almost always looks like a catastrophe in the making. It has a weak, foolish quality about it. We see this vividly acted out in the life of Gideon. Gideon's story is found in the sixth chapter of the Book of Judges. The nation of Israel was suffering terrible oppression at the hands of the Midianites. The people cried out to the Lord for deliverance and, in answer to their pleas, He commissioned Gideon to lead Israel to victory.

But Gideon appeared to be a very cowardly man. He was scared to death of the marauding Midianites and hid in the mountains and caves along with the rest of the children of Israel. He was also the "runt" in one of the poorest families in Manasseh.

Yet, God saw things differently. When the Angel of the Lord appeared to Gideon, He greeted him with these strange words: "'The LORD is with you, mighty warrior'" (v. 12). Even though God knew Gideon was a poor man and the least in his father's house, these were the qualities the Lord was looking for. Gideon's strength was not to be found in his own resources but in the acknowledgment of his weakness. The fact that God commissioned him would be the only authority he needed!

So, Gideon assembled a rugged group of farmers and peasants numbering about 32,000. They came with sticks, slingshots, and plowshares sharpened into spears. They weren't very impressive, to say the least. In contrast, the Midianites were skillful, ruthless warriors. They had state-of-the-art weaponry and an army of 135,000 men. They were hungry for a fight and looking for any excuse they could find to demonstrate their prowess.

But God told Gideon that he had way too many men. So He instructed Gideon to send all the fearful ones home. 22,000 men packed their bags, and 10,000 stayed. God then told Gideon that he still had too many men, and so he sifted through the ranks again, choosing soldiers on the basis of how they drank water from a brook. By the time Gideon was done, there were only 300 men remaining.

Then the Lord told Gideon one more thing: "Don't take any weapons! Each man is to go up against the Midianites bearing only a torch, a clay jar, and a horn." With nothing more than these odd "weapons of war," 300 men went out to meet the Midianites. Israel's enemies were overwhelmed, and they scattered in utter confusion. What an amazing victory! In the end, 300 peasants were chosen, not to display their might or strength but to demonstrate that, in *weakness*, God would be honored.

THE STRENGTH OF A SONG

A great army consisting of the children of Ammon, Moab, and Mount Seir had gathered together to attack Jerusalem. Jehoshaphat immediately assembled the people and the priests together, and they earnestly sought the Lord for guidance and help. King Jehoshaphat then stood before the people and cried out to God: "…For we have no power to face this vast army that is attacking us. We do not know what to do, but our eyes are upon you" (2 Chronicles 20:12).

Suddenly, the spirit of prophecy came upon a certain Levite of the sons of Asaph, and he stood and revealed the exact location of the enemy. He also gave the people specific instructions as to what they were to do: "'You will not have to fight this battle. Take up your positions; stand firm and see the deliverance the LORD will give you, O Judah and Jerusalem'" (v. 17).

Jehoshaphat sent "worshippers" ahead of the army and they sang, "'Give thanks to the LORD, for his love endures forever'" (v. 21). Confusion spread throughout the enemy's camp, and they destroyed each other! The only thing the people of Judah and Jerusalem had to do was gather the spoils. The "weakness of God," displayed through *singing*, overpowered the might of an entire army!

Many other examples can be found in the Bible that graphically illustrate God's willingness to demonstrate His power and wisdom through "instruments of weakness." A *rugged stick* in the hands of Moses became the *rod of God* that brought deliverance to the Hebrew people! Even a donkey was used as the mouthpiece of the Lord to talk to a misguided prophet by the name of Balaam.

Speaking of donkeys, Messiah would one day make His triumphal entrance into Jerusalem riding on a lowly burro (Matthew 21:1-11). This mode of transportation would mirror the humility and lowliness of the King of Kings who would be slain as an innocent lamb for the sins of the world.

GOD—A HELPLESS BABY, A CRUCIFIED "CRIMINAL"

The greatest display of God's *humility* and *weakness* was exhibited in the birth and death of His Son. In the story of Jesus' birth,

Omnipotence was clothed in the skin of fragile humanity! "The Word became flesh and made his dwelling among us" (John 1:14). The Word became a squirming baby lying in a feeding trough for cattle. This defenseless Child was born to a humble couple who carried the stigma of having a baby out of wedlock. But in the wisdom of God, this frail baby who nursed on the breasts of a teenage, virgin girl, would one day bruise the serpent's head (Genesis 3:15) and wreak havoc on the powers of darkness!

With the world in the grip of Satan and sin, God came disguised as an infant born in a stable to an unmarried couple. He lived in obscurity for 30 years, and then traveled throughout the various villages with a ragtag group of men. He became the opponent of the religious elite and was eventually crucified naked and condemned as a common criminal.

But beneath the disguises, we find true wisdom revealed. Again, Paul speaks of this in 1 Corinthians 1:21-25:

> *For since in the wisdom of God the world through its wisdom did not know him, God was pleased through the foolishness of what was preached to save those who believe. Jews demand miraculous signs and Greeks look for wisdom, but we preach Christ crucified: a stumbling block and foolishness to Gentiles, but to those whom God has called, both Jews and Greeks, Christ the power of God and the wisdom of God. For the foolishness of God is wiser than man's wisdom, and the weakness of God is stronger than man's strength (italics added).*

Satan had feared the young carpenter who had been walking around Galilee and Jerusalem preaching, healing, confronting hypocrites, and forgiving sins. He knew he had to deal with Jesus decisively. So he won the religious power brokers over to his side and provoked the Romans to take action. He made them feel resentful and angry until they all agreed that Jesus had to die.

Satan then laid a trap for the Son of God, and He walked right into it, *seemingly* unaware of what was taking place. He entered the snare alone, unarmed, and vulnerable. He didn't even put up a struggle. Like a lamb to the slaughter, Jesus was beaten and bruised, then nailed to a cross. He yielded to death, and it was finished!

But what was finished? And, who was finished? Paul gives us the answers in Colossians 2:15: "And having disarmed the powers and authorities, He made a public spectacle of them, triumphing over them by the Cross." The very thing that looked like a tragedy turned into triumph.

"The Cross was the devil's Trojan horse, the gift he seized that undid him."[36] He thought it was his trump card to secure his power over the world. But in the wisdom of God, the Cross turned out to be the thing that would destroy the adversary's works (1 John 3:8). The death of a *lamb* broke Satan's grip on us and delivered us from sin!

OUR MODEL FOR MEEKNESS

Undoubtedly, the greatest example of meekness was Jesus Himself. Humility was the lens through which He viewed all of His surroundings. It affected His perception, as well as His attitude, toward everything. Paul reiterated this for us in Philippians 2:5-8:

> *Have this attitude in yourselves which was also in Christ Jesus, who, although He existed in the form of God, did not regard equality with God a thing to be grasped, but emptied himself, taking the form of a bondservant, and being made in the likeness of men. And being found in appearance as a man, He humbled himself by becoming obedient to the point of death, even death on a cross"* (NASB).

What did Paul mean when he wrote that Jesus "emptied himself"? In theological terms, this is referred to as Christ's *kenosis* or "self-emptying" and is derived from the Greek term which occurs in this verse. According to this passage, it's apparent that Jesus

---

36 Buchanan, Mark. *The Holy Wild* (Sisters, OR: Multnomah Publishers, Inc., 2003), 132.

emptied Himself of His divine privileges. This doesn't mean that He gave up His divinity; it simply means that He voluntarily gave up the honor that was due Him as God.

In emptying Himself, Jesus modeled the nature of God by taking on the role of a servant. Think about it—

> What if Jesus' humility, meekness and servant heart were never a departure from God's glory and power, but actually define it and demonstrate it? Take your time—read that sentence again. What if kenosis—self-emptying power, self-giving love and radical servant-hood—expresses the very nature of God! What if God does rule and reign, not through imperial power but through kenotic love! What if the first beatitude—"Blessed are the poor (void, empty) in spirit; theirs is the kingdom of heaven" (Matt. 5:3)—is a vision of the glory of God lived through Christ! Why? Wherever God, wherever Christ, wherever we risk emptying ourselves of self-will and self-rule to make space for the other, that is where the supernatural kingdom-love of God rules and reigns. Thus, kenosis, which is to say love (!), is the heart of who God is. Not lording over, but always coming under; not triumphing through conquest, but through the Cross. God's being and God's power are his kenotic love.[37]

For Christ to empty Himself, He gave up the privilege of being *somebody*. Although He did make something of His life, He did it through humility and servanthood. He willingly chose to serve dying humanity and "...give His life as a ransom for many" (Matthew 20:28).

As a humble Savior, Jesus also gave up the right to be *respected*. We're reminded again in verse eight that "...He humbled himself by becoming obedient to the point of death, even death on a cross." And what a humiliating death it was. Jesus was crucified between two thieves. The association with these criminals left no doubt as to what His accusers thought of Him. This was death in its worst form! Crucifixion was a slow and excruciating execution used by

37 Jersak, Bradley. *A More Christlike God* (Pasadena, CA: CWRpress, 2015), 100-101.

Rome to deter crime. People were brought face to face with all
the gore of the moment. They would come and mock those being
punished, venting their anger on the ones who had committed
crimes against society.

Jesus could have easily destroyed His enemies. But He was not
threatened by the attempts of His accusers to make Him nothing.
He had given up the right to demand respect. The restraint required
for the Creator of the universe to allow human beings to deliberately end His life is beyond imagination. The Lord's meekness
constituted the mightiest power the world has ever known!

Although Jesus was a King, it was not beneath Him to embrace the role of a slave. Though He was rich, He was content in
not having a place to lay His head. Though His hands formed the
universe, He chose to wash the dirty feet of mere mortals. Instead
of requiring those around Him to bow down and give Him the
respect He deserved, He invited them to walk with Him and call
Him friend.

Jesus "stripped" Himself of His divine privileges and, while
hanging on the Cross, *exposed* the most *vulnerable* parts of the
Godhead to humanity. And He did it all because He knew this is
what would be necessary for us to understand and experience an
authentic relationship with His Father.

Think of it. This was how *low* God was willing to stoop for
our redemption. This one act of divine service for humanity is
unparalleled in history! Maybe this is why the late German New
Testament scholar Martin Hengel wrote,

> The discrepancy between the shameful death of a Jewish
> state criminal and the confession that depicts this executed
> man as the pre-existent divine figure who becomes man and
> humbles himself to a slave's death is, as far as I can see, without
> analogy in the ancient world.[38]

---

38 Hengel, Martin. *The Son of God: The Origin of Christology and the History
   of Jewish-Hellenistic Religion*, trans. John Bowden (Philadelphia: Fortress,
   1976), 1.

The more we understand God's *ways*, the more we'll come to realize that He truly is the embodiment of *humility*. The anonymous Eastern monk who wrote the book, *Jesus, a Dialogue with the Saviour*, said it best:

> We are accustomed to thinking of the Father in terms of power. Yes, the Father is omnipotent. But the Father's heart is meek and humble like the Saviour's....He attaches no importance to display or appearances. He prefers the poor means and is united to the voluntary abasement of His Son who took on our nature and suffering. We must learn to see the Father in this light.[39]

BEARING HIS IMAGE

As we reflect on the personality and character of God, we soon discover there's something that takes place in us that's absolutely transforming. The more we embrace His heart, the more we start bearing His image. Maybe this is why Paul wrote, "Your attitude should be the same as that of Christ Jesus" (Philippians 2:5).

As human beings, we spend a great deal of time and energy trying to make something of ourselves. We are constantly surrounded by messages that drive us to be self-motivated. "You only go around once in life!" "Just do it!" "Be all that you can be!" Because we're always encouraged to seek self-recognition, the *way* of weakness and humility presents a real crisis in our lives. The reason for this should not be difficult for us to understand. Only by embracing the mind of Christ can we even submit to such a life of meekness.

God never calls any of us to a life of mediocrity. He wants us to be spiritually motivated in all that we do. But the attitude of humility is always essential for the purifying of our motives. What are our ambitions? What are our goals? For example, if we have come to like the power and influence of a particular career or ministry, we need to surrender them to the Lord, recognizing that they are His, not ours.

---

39 *Jesus, a Dialogue with the Saviour*, by a monk of the Eastern Church, (New York: Desclee, 1962), 134-135.

We are extremely vulnerable when our identity and fulfillment come from sources other than our relationship with our heavenly Father. This is why we need to remind ourselves that everything originates from Him and we are merely His stewards. Father has entrusted us with gifts, talents, resources, and relationships which we are responsible for managing and developing. But we will never be able to fully bear His image until we stop trying to promote ourselves with the gifts, talents, resources, and relationships that have only been loaned to us.

If we are going to truly experience the life and nature of Jesus, we must hold back nothing from Him. He who gave everything invites us to give Him everything. Even the closest things to our hearts, including our *reputations*, must be brought to Christ.

There was a time in the life of Charles Haddon Spurgeon when he was subjected to slander and criticism because of his passion for Jesus and his desire to take the gospel to the people. This eloquent British preacher said in a sermon in 1857,

> I shall never forget the circumstance when, after I thought I had made a full consecration to Christ, a slanderous report against my character came to my ears, and my heart was broken in agony because I should have to lose that (his reputation), in preaching Christ's Gospel. I fell on my knees, and said, 'Master, I will not keep back even my character from Thee. If I must lose that too, then let it go; it is the dearest thing I have; but it shall go, if, like my Master, they shall say that I have a devil, and am mad.'[40]

It is certainly much easier to *confess* Christ than it is to follow Him. The thought of being broken and weak in the eyes of others troubles us. We want to manage our lives because we don't know what Jesus will require of us. Yet we are never really free until we've taken our hands off the controls of our lives and given up the right to defend ourselves.

---

40 Wood, Arthur Skevington. *Baptised with Fire* (London: Pickering and Inglis, 1981), 79.

Years ago, there was a minister who had a congregation that continually refused to accept his message. He wanted to lead the people into a knowledge of Christ, but they were unwilling to follow. Whenever he stood up to preach, he felt as if the adversary were standing next to him, resisting him. Things became so bad that he even had to ask the choir to resign. The choir not only resigned but also persuaded the rest of the congregation to stop singing. From that point on, the only singing was done by the preacher.

One day, as he found himself at his wit's end, the Lord spoke to him through an odd set of circumstances. He was sitting on a park bench when he saw part of a newspaper lying on the ground. As he looked at the torn piece of paper, his eyes fell on these words: "No man is ever fully accepted until he has, first of all, been utterly rejected." For him, this was all that needed to be said. He had been completely rejected by man, but the recognition of the fact that he was fully accepted by God began a period of fruitful ministry in another area that lasted for years.

When we truly trust our heavenly Father, we can surrender our right to be respected. We don't have to defend ourselves. If we're willing to bear His image and embrace the *way* of weakness and humility, He will take over our public relations.

> *To this you were called, because Christ suffered for you, leaving you an example, that you should follow in his steps. 'He committed no sin, and no deceit was found in his mouth.' When they hurled their insults at him, he did not retaliate; when He suffered, He made no threats. Instead, he entrusted himself to him who judges justly* (1 Peter 2:21-23).

We're also told in Philippians 2:9-11 that because Jesus emptied Himself of His divine privileges and became obedient to death,

> *...God exalted him to the highest place and gave him the name that is above every name, that at the name of Jesus every knee should bow, in heaven, and on earth, and under*

*the earth, and every tongue confess that Jesus Christ is Lord,
to the glory of God the Father.*

The *broken* Savior who willingly became the least has become the
greatest!

If we're willing to embrace the attitude of Christ, He will
use us in His time and in His way. The path to *promotion* in the
kingdom of God doesn't come by how much we can obtain, or
how big we can get, or how far we can go. Rather, true promotion
only comes as we're willing to bear the Lord's image in our lives.
We can only impart life to others as our lives reflect the humility
of our broken Savior.

THE CRACKED POT

A water-bearer in India had two large pots. Each hung
on opposite ends of a pole that he carried across his neck. One
of the pots had a crack in it, while the other was perfect. The
latter always delivered a full portion of water at the end of the
long walk from the stream to the master's house. The cracked
pot arrived only half-full. Every day for a full two years, the
water-bearer delivered only one and a half pots of water.

The perfect pot was proud of its accomplishments, because it fulfilled magnificently the purpose for which it had
been made. But the poor cracked pot was ashamed of its im-
perfections, miserable that it was able to accomplish only half
of what it had been made to do.

After the second year of what it perceived to be a bitter
failure, the unhappy pot spoke to the water-bearer one day by
the stream.

"I am ashamed of myself, and I want to apologize to you,"
the pot said.

"Why?" asked the bearer. "What are you ashamed of?"

"I have been able, for these past two years, to deliver only
half my load, because this crack in my side causes water to leak
out all the way back to your master's house."

The water-bearer felt sorry for the old cracked pot, and in
his compassion, he said, "As we return to the master's house,

I want you to notice the beautiful flowers along the path." Indeed, as they went up the hill, the cracked pot took notice of the beautiful wildflowers on the side of the path, bright in the sun's glow, and the sight cheered it up a bit.

But at the end of the trail, it still felt bad that it had leaked out half its load, and so again it apologized to the bearer for its failure.

The bearer said to the pot, "Did you notice that there were flowers only on your side of the path, not on the other pot's side?... I planted flower seeds on your side of the path, and every day, as we have walked back from the stream, you have watered them. For two years I have been able to pick these beautiful flowers to decorate my master's table. Without you being just the way you are, he would not have had this beauty to grace his house."[41]

A CRAFT CALLED KINTSUKUROI

In Japan there is a craft called Kintsukuroi. This Japanese word literally means "to repair with gold." Kintsukuroi is the art of repairing broken pottery with gold or silver lacquer in order to make the vessel even more beautiful for having been broken.

The art of Kintsukuroi vividly illustrates what our heavenly Father does with the brokenness of our world. He takes the pieces of our shattered lives and gently crafts them into vessels that make us an even more beautiful reflection of His glory than we ever were before!

Father God understands you and your *world* better than anyone else you will ever know. He is patiently making you into who He planned you to be from the beginning. He will never leave you or turn His back on you. He's in it for the long haul! He cares about the end of your "story," and He's wholeheartedly committed to it.

---

41 Manning, Brennan. *Ruthless Trust* (Harper San Francisco, CA: 2000), 133-135.

6 AFFECTIONATE—NOT ANGRY

Did God get a makeover between the Old and New Testaments? At first glance, it appears that He may have. While much of the Old Testament *seems* to portray Him as angry and vengeful, the revelation that Jesus unveiled in the New Testament appears to introduce us to a more gracious God. So, what are we to think?

When coming face to face with some of the graphic language of the Old Testament, we seemingly encounter "horror" stories of God killing the firstborn of Egypt and raining down fire from heaven to consume Sodom and Gomorrah. God even appeared so unapproachable that the most "righteous" individuals fell on their faces, paralyzed by fear.

No wonder we've been somewhat confused when we turn to the New Testament and note that Jesus clearly stated that to see Him is to see the Father (John 14:9). And then He proceeded to go into homes and eat with outcasts, forgive murderers and prostitutes, heal the sick, and invite children to crawl up on His lap. He portrayed His Father as so kind and tender that even the most immoral individual could run into His arms and feel His embrace.

So, is God loving and gracious one moment and angry and vengeful the next? Many of us have been taught that He's both, and that's why we struggle having confidence in His feelings for us. We often try to figure out if we're in or out of His favor, and we end up on an emotional rollercoaster ride. This "He loves me, He loves me not" way of thinking is a vicious cycle that offers us no hope or resolution.

Until we are willing to tackle some of the tough issues *primarily* related to the "God of the Old Testament," we will never really

have a cohesive view of His character. But this may not be easy
for some of us to do. None of us is completely objective when it
comes to our belief systems. We all have various biases. And, over
the years, it has been easy for us to slip into *dogmatic presumptions*
over traditional views of God's nature that have influenced our
thinking. But the important thing is to recognize our biases and
be willing to defend them when we can and honestly challenge
them when we can't.

I think all of us would agree that God didn't undergo a radical
makeover between the Testaments! Yet, what we often fail to understand is that before Jesus came to earth, men could only see God's
actions through their "primitive" lenses. But Jesus changed the way
men perceived God. He came to earth as the perfect reflection of
the Godhead (Colossians 1:15; 2:9). He fully expressed the heart
of His Father so we might know Him as He really is and no longer
be victims of our own *misunderstandings*.

When we look at how Jesus lived and reflect on His words,
we have to be reminded that all of our thinking about God must
be rooted in Christ! Jesus is the *Logos*, the Word of God revealed
in the Scriptures. He showed us what God has always been like
(John 14:8-9). In fact, in John 1:18, we read that "No one has
ever seen God; but the only and unique Son, who is identical with
God and is at the Father's side—he has made him known" (CJB).
This was written by a Jew who knew the scriptural traditions of his
forefathers. And, he emphatically stated that the Jewish patriarchs
and prophets such as Abraham, Moses, David, and Elijah had not
perceived or understood God in a completely accurate way. While
they had encounters with God, they didn't know and experience
Him as He fully is.

As Dr. Stephen Crosby has pointed out,

> The Jewish patriarchs perceived things only in shadowy
> form as Paul (also a Jew) said (Col 2:17)! The substance is only
> in Christ!...Christ is the interpretation of Scripture. He is our
> standard and measure. Our understanding and application
> of Old Testament Scripture must be ***adopted***, ***adapted***, or

rejected based on what we see in the life and ministry of Jesus Christ."[42]

In other words, we need to read and study the Scriptures through the "lens" of Jesus.

While I'm convinced the ideas presented in this chapter may help answer some of the difficult questions you may have had over the years, I'm also fully aware that the *weighty subjects* that will be addressed can't be thoroughly examined in such a limited amount of space. But despite the fact that I can't begin to answer all of your questions (I still have some of my own), I hope that the principles you're introduced to in the following pages will encourage you to *explore* the depths and riches of God's character like never before and challenge you to *wrestle* with the *mysteries* of the Scriptures!

RETHINKING OUR THINKING

In embarking on a quest to bring some clarity to the apparent theological tension between the revelation of God unveiled in the Old Covenant and the truth of God's nature revealed in Christ, we first need to be reminded that the Old Testament was an *incomplete* revelation of God's nature. While inspired, it was still a progressive unfolding of God's heart and will that would see its fulfillment in the coming of Messiah. One of the primary reasons why Jesus came to earth was to give us a true picture and understanding of the character of God.

Furthermore, to understand some of the language of the Old Testament, we need to be aware of the belief systems of both ancient Israel and the cultures that influenced them.

For example, it was *common* in ancient Near Eastern worship to find sacrifices, a priesthood, holy places, circumcision, purification rites, and festivals. In his providence, God appropriated certain symbols and rituals familiar to Israel and infused them with new meaning and significance in light of

---

42 Crosby, Dr. Stephen. *How New is the New Covenant* (Stephanos Ministries, 2016), 89.

his saving, historical acts and his covenant relationship with Israel (italics added).[43]

God worked with the Hebrew people as He found them. He used language and illustrations they could understand. He met them where they were while seeking to show them a higher ideal in the context of ancient Near Eastern life. We can't make sense of their views until we set them against their background and environment. For example, while being enslaved in Egypt for 400 years, Israel had been introduced to the worship of many *gods*. Since one of the prevailing views of that time period depicted the earth as being founded on and encircled by water, some of the most powerful, tyrannical *gods* were thought to be those of the sea.

One of those *gods* was the "sea lord" Yamm. Yamm (the Canaanite/Phoenician sea god) was adopted into Egyptian worship and viewed as a very volatile god of the waters. In a passage that many scholars believe mentions Yamm by name, the psalmist wrote, "How long will the enemy mock you, O God? Will the foe revile your name forever...? It was you who split open the sea [yām] by your power; you broke the heads of the monster in the waters" (Psalm 74:10, 13).[44]

This passage seems to identify Yamm with "the monster in the waters," and this monster is clearly an enemy of Yahweh. Similar references to Yamm may possibly be found in Job 9:8 which depicted Yahweh treading on the waves of the sea. Habakkuk 3:8-15 also portrayed God's "...rage against the sea" [yām] that "...roared and lifted its waves on high" (vs. 8, 10). The writer later declared, "You trampled the sea [yām] with your horses, churning the great waters" (v. 15).

These verses in Habakkuk appear to be referring to the historic deliverance of the Hebrew people out of Egypt (v. 13). Isaiah 51:9-11 also pictured God's emancipation of the children of Israel

---

43 Ross, Allen P. *Holiness to the Lord* (Grand Rapids, MI: Baker Academic, 2006).

44 The thoughts in this section were inspired by Gregory A. Boyd, *God At War* (Downers Grove, IL: InterVarsity Press, 1997), 87-88.

through the Red Sea as a type of Yahweh's triumphant battle over Yamm. Isaiah first proclaimed how God "...cut Rahab to pieces" and "...pierced the monster through" (v. 9). In some passages, Rahab appears to be just another name for Yamm. Isaiah then continued by declaring that it was Yahweh who "...dried up the sea" [yām] and therefore, "...made the depths of the sea a road for the redeemed to cross over" (v. 10).

The prophet Isaiah saw the parting of the Red Sea as a great victory for Yahweh over Yamm. Because God could've delivered His people from Egypt a different way, Jews came to believe that the primary reason He split the Sea was to demonstrate that He was the *only* true God and that He was more powerful than the "sea gods" of the surrounding nations.

Also, according to Jewish thinking, the parting of the Red Sea appears to have been a sign to the "mixed multitude" who marched out of Egypt with the Hebrew people (Exodus 12:38). Some scholars believe that these *strangers* were native Egyptians who were frightened by the plagues and were anxious to escape the tyranny of the kings. Others suggest that these people were the remains of the old Semitic population of the eastern provinces. It has even been thought that the "mixed multitude" consisted of fugitives from other races who had been oppressed by the pharaohs. Whoever these individuals were, it's safe to assume they came from cultures that believed in the worship of various *gods* (polytheism). Many of them were probably carrying their idols with them as they departed the land of Egypt. It was against this backdrop that Israel came to understand that God divided the waters of the Red Sea to wean the multitude from their polytheism and to *awe* them with His power!

Throughout the Old Testament, God was laying the groundwork for a progressive revelation of Himself that would culminate in the coming of Messiah. The focal point of this foundation was monotheism (the belief in only one God). Because of the polytheistic views of Israel's neighbors, God was consistently emphasizing that He alone is Creator and that He alone is the sovereign Ruler of the whole world. Given this emphasis, the Hebrew writers of Scripture often described events or circumstances as coming from the hand of their Creator. But as we look at the Old Testament through the lens of Christ, it soon becomes apparent that God did not mean that every event was caused or ordained by Him.

This principle is vividly illustrated for us in the story of the plagues that descended on Egypt. In Exodus 12:12, we are told that God was going to pass through the land and strike all the firstborn of Egypt, both men and animals. But within the space of twelve verses, we read that He promised to protect those who covered their doorposts in lamb's blood by not *allowing* "the destroyer" to come into their houses and kill them (v. 23).

So how do we reconcile the apparent disparity between verses 12 and 23? First of all, Lamentations 3:33 tells us that God "… does not willingly bring affliction or grief to the children of men." This verse is just one of many which reinforces the truth that God does *not* cause or ordain evil. He never wants anyone to suffer devastation and destruction. Instead, He "longs to be gracious" to everyone (Isaiah 30:18) and invites mankind to turn to Him (Isaiah 65:1-2; Ezekiel 18:23, 30-32; Hosea 11:8-9; Romans 10:21; 1 Timothy 2:4). From these passages, as well as Exodus 12:23, it's clear that God was not the source of Egypt's calamity; instead, the *destroyer* was able to torment the people and kill their firstborn as a result of generations of sin and idolatry.

These truths are further reinforced by the Apostle Paul in 1 Corinthians 10:8-11. Reflecting on the accounts of Israel committing harlotry with the daughters of Moab (Numbers 25:1-9), grumbling against the Lord (Numbers 21:6-9), and rebelling against the leadership of Moses (Numbers 16), Paul wrote,

> *Nor let us commit sexual immorality, as some of them did, and in one day twenty-three thousand fell; nor let us tempt Christ, as some of them also tempted, and were destroyed by serpents; nor complain, as some of them also complained, and were destroyed by the destroyer. Now all*

these things happened to them as examples, and they were written for our admonition, upon whom the ends of the ages have come" (NKJV).

Paul clearly stated that due to the sins of the people, serpents, as well as the destroyer, were able to devastate their lives.

Although Paul was citing passages from the Old Testament that emphatically declared God was the source of the plagues, Paul assigned the destruction to the destroyer! According to the Apostle Paul, when wrath was revealed, God was not the destroyer—Satan was!

Second, it's imperative that we understand how God addresses the issue of man's sin. Because there is so much erroneous teaching about the subject of *judgment*, it's absolutely essential that we properly interpret the nature of God's wrath. The Lord has always "judged" sin by *allowing* people to experience the consequences of their wrong choices. Since God ultimately defines what *true reality* is and what is best for mankind, when people resist this *reality*, they inevitably bring suffering and destruction on themselves.

We can see this clearly lived out in God's *unique* relationship with Israel. The Old Testament depicted the Lord as a wounded Husband who frequently attempted to woo His wayward wife back to Himself (Isaiah 54:5-6; Jeremiah 2:2; Ezekiel 6:7-8; Hosea 2:14-16). He was deeply troubled over her spiritual condition and her repeated unfaithfulness. God's *pure jealousy* was expressed in His continual warnings to His wife that if she persisted in giving herself to other lovers, she would eventually be destroyed as a result of her ungodly choices. Through the prophets, the Lord warned Israel because He wanted to protect the intimacy they had with each other and because He wanted to defend their marriage.

The prophets never thought of "God's wrath" as something that was irrational, out of control, or unpredictable. While the words *anger* and *wrath* naturally denote recklessness and spite, the biblical terms convey the idea of *righteous indignation*. In other words, God can't be impartial to evil. And, neither can He be indifferent. It's because He cares so deeply for man that He is profoundly pained and utterly upset by the nature of sin and injustice. By having to *allow* men to suffer the consequences of their wrong choices, it grieves Him that sin is able to wreak havoc on the world.

While God is the sovereign King of the universe, He has to "honor" the free choices of human beings. He does so because of the way He has designed things within the created order. He has to allow men and women the freedom to choose what they want even though He knows there will eventually be dire consequences for the wrong decisions they make. But it has always been His desire that men turn to Him in their distress.

We read in John 3:17-19,

> *For God did not send his Son into the world to condemn the world, but to save the world through him. Whoever believes in him is not condemned, but whoever does not believe stands condemned already because he has not believed in the name of God's one and only Son. This is the verdict: Light has come into the world, but men loved darkness instead of light because their deeds were evil.*

The Apostle James also understood that those who reject the source of love and beauty end up actually choosing *loveless living* and misery. He knew that the ugly consequences of sin are the natural results of their wrong decisions. And this is why he wrote:

> *When tempted, no one should say, 'God is tempting me.' For God cannot be tempted by evil, nor does he tempt anyone; but each one is tempted when, by his own evil desire, he is dragged away and enticed. Then, after desire has conceived, it gives birth to sin, and sin, when it is full-grown, gives birth to death* (James 1:13-15).

Furthermore, Paul taught that the "wrath of God" revealed from heaven (Romans 1:18) was actually the Lord letting ungodly men have their own way. He "…let them go ahead and do whatever shameful things their hearts desired," and "...abandoned them to their evil minds and let them do things that should never be done" (vs. 24, 28, NLT).

In Romans 5:8-9, Paul supported his position even more: "But God demonstrates His own love toward us, in that while we were yet sinners, Christ died for us. Much more then, having now been justified by His blood, we shall be saved from the wrath *of God* through Him" (NASB). Commenting on these verses, Dr. Bradley Jersak has written,

> Did you notice the italicized phrase 'of God' inserted there?...The italicized phrase "of God" in the New American Standard Bible is the translators' way of letting you know they added the phrase. No manuscript includes those words. The verse literally ends, "we shall be saved through him from the wrath." Translators add "God's wrath," or, "wrath from God" or "wrath of God," because, they say, it is understood. Other translations, like the New International Version, insert "of God" without any indication that they placed it there, either in italics or a marginal note. They assume it belongs.
>
> God's wrath is understood? Really? By whom? And why? The translators' assumption is that they can and should insert the words, 'of God,' though they are not found in the manuscripts, nor implied by the grammar. We are to accept the translators' own interpretation, passed on to readers, that Paul meant Jesus saves us from the wrath of God, even though Paul certainly did not say 'wrath of God.' Neither, I would suggest, is that his meaning in context.
>
> What Paul actually says is that God through Christ was saving us from the wrath. Period. We are not to believe that Jesus is saving us from God the Father, but from the consequences intrinsic to sin itself, namely death.[45]

The Lord has never delighted in judgment. He understands that the world is dark and that human agony is unbearable. So in what does He delight? Jeremiah 9:24 sheds some light on the heart

---

45 Jersak, Bradley. *A More Christlike God* (Pasadena, CA: CWRpress, 2015), 208-209.

and mind of God. "...I am the LORD who is just and righteous, whose love is unfailing, and that I delight in these things. I, the LORD have spoken!" (NLT).

Still, what of those who challenge God: "...Is your permission—your giving over—not tantamount to complicity?"

And the answer, at some level, is probably yes. If not complicit, God has accepted ultimate responsibility as the First Cause of it all—such that some biblical authors do use the phrase 'wrath of God' to describe what are technically secondary consequences. Ultimately, this is God's good order and God is finally responsible for all that is, including intrinsic consequences for our abuse of freedom. I have called this wrath as giving over or wrath as cruciform consent.

Wrath as consent is the great and terrible price of God's plan and God's cruciform nature, but it is not the whole story. God has also chosen to redeem and restore the world through his love. Redeeming the world through love, instead of taking it by violent conquest, means allowing horrible things to happen that, from our limited human perspective, make God look both wrathful and weak all at once. The cognitive dissonance (i.e., 'brain freeze') we feel cannot be resolved rationally. Instead, we have looked in wonder to the Cross—a tree of love and life, not a tree of keen arguments and answers. On that Cross, we witness God's nonviolent consent.

God's nonviolent consent extends to the whole of natural and spiritual reality. It includes nonviolent consent to human freedom, for good or ill. It includes nonviolent consent to the laws of nature, for beauty or tragedy, creation or destruction. It includes nonviolent consent to spiritual laws of sowing and reaping, blessing and cursing....

The Lamb slain from the foundation of the world died to being all-powerful before Creation. This kenotic self-renunciation has made space for creation. For freedom and for violence. For genocide and hurricanes and car accidents and pedophiles.

But also for love.[46]

---

46 Ibid., 210-211.

Third, because of the Lord's *passionate* love for man, He has always taken personal responsibility for all that He allows, even though He detests much of what He has to allow. When we look at the Old Testament in particular, we find God frequently identifying Himself as the agent of violence, though the context of Scripture makes it clear that He is merely allowing "violent agents" to do what they want to do. For example, this is explicitly illustrated in the crucifixion of Christ. "According to Isaiah 53:10, the Father is said to have afflicted His Son; but, in fact, He merely allowed *wicked agents* using wicked people to crucify Jesus."[47]

Fourth, as a hermeneutical rule, we should always interpret the Old Testament in light of the New Testament, and not vice versa. If Jesus' ministry taught us anything, it demonstrated that "natural" occurrences such as earthquakes, volcanoes, and even life-threatening storms are either the *direct* or *indirect* result of Satan's activity. Far from revealing God's character, such "natural" phenomena expose the character of His *archenemy*.

Sin energizes evil! And, evil can have a devastating effect on nature. We see this powerfully portrayed in the destruction of Sodom and Gomorrah. According to Genesis 19:24, the Lord rained down fire and brimstone from heaven and destroyed these cities because of the sins of the people. But, in reality, scientists have discovered that at one time there was major volcanic activity under the Dead Sea. Because the cities of Sodom and Gomorrah were located on the coastal regions of the Dead Sea, they were destroyed as a result of a massive volcanic eruption. While the storyline suggests that this event was an act of God, it was actually the *destroyer* who wreaked havoc on the region as a consequence of the people's sins, and Sodom and Gomorrah ended up reeling under the weight of volcanic lava!

Christ's entire ministry reflected the view that the world had been seized by a sinister adversary, and He had come to take it back. Contrary to the view that everything has a divine purpose behind it, He demonstrated that His Father's purposes for the planet had

---

47 Taken from Gregory A. Boyd's blog, November 8, 2009.

to be fought for and won. Jesus taught His disciples to pray that God's will would be done "on earth as it is in heaven" (Matthew 6:10). This suggests that, to a significant extent, God's will is not being accomplished on the earth right now. The planet is still a war zone and, sadly, there are real-life casualties!

In principle, Jesus defeated Satan through the Cross and established His Father's kingdom on earth (Colossians 2:14-15; Hebrews 2:14; 1 John 3:8). But the New Testament does not infer that the adversary has ceased wreaking havoc on this world. This is the paradox of the "already, not yet" tension we find in the New Testament. While Satan has *already* been defeated by Christ, His victory has *not yet* been fully realized on the earth. Therefore, it's the primary calling of the Church to apply Christ's victory to the world in spite of the violent opposition it faces.

Furthermore, if the violent state of the planet reveals God's design and is "natural" as some teach, why does the Bible promise that such violence will disappear when the Lord's kingdom is fully established (Isaiah 11:6-9; 65:25)? These passages clearly suggest that when everything is brought into perfect harmony with God's will, there will be no evil or violence. But for now, much of creation is still under the influence of "violent beings" who oppose God's design. All evil originates in the will of self-determining creatures, and that's why it can't be traced back to God!

Other Perplexing Passages

There are also a number of other "perplexing passages" in the Old Testament that seem to stand at odds against the nature of God's love revealed in Christ. In this section, I want to highlight just a few of these verses to try to bring some clarity concerning their meaning. One such passage is found in ***Exodus 4:11***: "'Who gave man his mouth? Who makes him deaf or mute? Who gives him sight or makes him blind? Is it not I, the LORD?'" According to some individuals, this verse clearly teaches that all infirmities are willed by God.[48] But this interpretation is flawed for several reasons. First of all, as we've mentioned previously, all of our ideas about God must be summed up in the person of Jesus Christ. Throughout His ministry, Jesus consistently rebuked infirmities and diseases as evidence that they were not His Father's will. Furthermore, Christ never encouraged anyone to take comfort in the idea that these things were a part of some "divine design."

Second, it's important to read this verse in context. Moses was complaining to God about His decision to send him as His spokesperson to Pharaoh on the grounds that he was "slow of speech and tongue" (Exodus 4:10). God became understandably frustrated with Moses and, therefore, used emphatic language to drive home the point that, as Creator, He could handle every obstacle that stood in the way of delivering the Hebrew slaves out of Egypt. Thus, He rhetorically asked Moses, "Who gave man his mouth? Who makes him deaf or mute?"

Third, this passage does not suggest that God picks and chooses which individuals will be deaf, mute, or blind. This verse only implies that He created a world in which human beings can become disabled. God wanted Moses to understand that, as Creator, He is able to overcome all such obstacles to achieve His purposes.

Another passage we want to examine is ***Exodus 7:3-4***, where God said, "'... I will harden Pharaoh's heart, and though I multiply my miraculous signs and wonders in Egypt, he will not listen to you.'" There are those who would argue that this verse vividly demonstrates God's absolute sovereignty over man, and that He hardens whomever He chooses (Romans 9:18). But, as we've already seen, it's difficult to reconcile this perception of God with the truth that He longs for everyone to turn to Him (Isaiah 30:18; Ezekiel 18:30-32; Romans 10:21; 2 Peter 3:9), that He "...does not willingly bring affliction or grief to the children of men" (Lamentations 3:33), and that evil springs from man's own heart (Matthew 15:19).

---

48 The thoughts in this section were inspired by Gregory A. Boyd, *Satan And The Problem Of Evil* (Downers Grove, IL: InterVarsity Press, 2001), 397.

Also, the Bible clearly demonstrates that Pharaoh had already hardened his heart and God *used* his wickedness to fulfill His own purposes. This principle is also reinforced in Proverbs 16:4: "The LORD works out everything for his own ends—even the wicked for a day of disaster." In other words, God *directs* the wickedness of individuals and nations so that their end eventually fits into His overall plans.

One of the other passages we need to look at is found in *Judges 9:23*: "God sent an evil spirit between Abimelech and the cities of Shechem, who acted treacherously against Abimelech." Some would argue that this verse supports the view that God always uses evil spirits to carry out His will. However, we need to note that the word "evil" can simply mean "troubling" or "disastrous." It doesn't have to refer to an evil spirit. Instead, this passage is likely suggesting that, as an act of judgment, God *allowed* a *troubling spirit* to harass Abimelech.

But even if it could be proven that the *spirit* in this verse was some evil entity, it doesn't justify the conclusion that evil spirits always carry out God's plans and purposes. If this were the case, we would have to believe that God was in conflict with Himself. How could Jesus rebuke and cast out demons by the power of the Holy Spirit if the evil spirits were *there* by the will of God? The Lord's kingdom, like Satan's kingdom, can't be at war with itself.

We also need to examine the language of *Isaiah 45:7*, where God said, "I form the light and create darkness, I bring prosperity and create disaster; I, the LORD, do all these things." This passage is similar to Lamentations 3:37-38: "Who can speak and have it happen if the Lord has not decreed it? Is it not from the mouth of the Most High that both calamities and good things come?" The Isaiah passage addressed the future deliverance of Israel out of Babylon.[49] As some theologians have argued, the "light" and "darkness" mentioned in this verse refer to "emancipation" and "enslavement" (Isaiah 9:1-2; Lamentations 3:2). The "prosperity" and "disaster" speak of the Lord's plan to bless His people and, at the same time,

---

49 Ibid., 410-411.

allow the people of Babylon to experience the disaster brought about by their own decisions.

In addition, if we read Lamentations 3:37-38 in context, these verses don't imply that God creates or ordains evil (See v. 33). This passage is not addressing His universal, sovereign activity; it's speaking specifically of prophecy. Both "good" and "bad" prophecies came from the mouth of the Lord. As much as it troubled Him, He had to prophesy judgments on Israel through the prophets because of human rights abuses (v. 34).

Finally, let's look at one last passage from the Old Testament found in ***Malachi 1:2-3***. The Lord said, "'…I have loved Jacob, but Esau I have hated.'" When we examine the context surrounding these verses, we discover that the nations of Israel and Edom were being addressed, as opposed to their individual ancestors, Jacob and Esau (See also Romans 9:6-13). God had chosen (loved) Israel and entered into a covenant relationship with the nation. The Jewish people were chosen to properly represent God in the earth and eventually usher in the coming of Messiah. On the other hand, Edom didn't have a covenant relationship with God and had not been chosen to fulfill the same purposes as Israel. So, in that sense, they were "hated."

However, when we study the word "hate" from an ancient Jewish perspective, we find that it simply means "loved less than." This truth is reinforced for us in Genesis 29:30-31: "And he went in also unto Rachel, and he loved also Rachel *more than* Leah, and served with him yet seven other years. And when the LORD saw that Leah was *hated*, he opened her womb: but Rachel was barren" (KJV, italics added). Jesus even reiterated this same idea when he stated in Luke 14:26 that if anyone was going to follow Him, they were going to have to "hate" their father, mother, wife and children, brothers and sisters, and even their own lives. But in the parallel passage found in Matthew 10:37, Christ clearly indicated that those who loved their families more than Him were not worthy of Him. In other words, in order to be His disciples, they would have to love their families "less than" Him.

In concluding this chapter, always remember that *love* is the very essence of who God is. And, as you've already discovered by now, the Old Testament contains countless numbers of pictures of a God who is rich in mercy, willing to forgive, and extremely passionate about setting people free from those things that could potentially destroy their lives!

7 BEHOLDING GOD

Centuries ago, an early Church leader by the name of Irenaeus made the following observation: "The glory of God is the human being fully alive." But in the less-quoted second part of his statement, he wrote, "And the life of the human consists in beholding God."[50]

In our modern Christian culture, the words of Irenaeus may seem foreign and outdated. As a result, many of us may not even be familiar with the truth he was trying to convey. While God may be somewhat real to us, we're not as *intrigued* by Him as we could be if we only knew what it was to live a life of "beholding Him." Our problem isn't that we don't love God; we're just often unaware of His presence and unfamiliar with His fascinating personality.

If we truly don't know what God is like and how He thinks and feels, we have no basis for celebrating Him and finding our ultimate satisfaction in Him. Joy in God can't take place in an intellectual vacuum. Our delight in Him is the result of what we know to be true about Him.

When our thoughts and ideas about God continue to grow, our fascination with Him will increase as well. As our understanding of God increases so, too, will our love and affection for Him. Fresh insights from the Scriptures will also help lead us to a greater awareness of who He really is and will fan the flames of love in our lives.

What this should suggest to us is that the *ultimate* goal of our study of the Scriptures is to *encounter* God, not just to acquire knowledge or achieve doctrinal accuracy. If our knowledge of God

---

50 Iranaeus, *Against Heresies*, Book 4, 20.7

doesn't lead us to a greater sense of awe and wonder and enable us to experience a greater degree of His manifest presence, then we have failed to understand the reason why He gave us the Scriptures in the first place.

So, what did Irenaeus mean by the phrase, "beholding God"? And did he honestly believe there was a correlation between our being fully alive as human beings and our *gazing on God*? Even the words themselves seem rather mystical. But, instead of appearing mysterious, *beholding God* should be as natural to us as breathing!

BIBLICAL MEDITATION

Beholding God is all about the practice of reflecting on the transcendent splendor and beauty of God revealed in Jesus, the Scriptures, and creation. It's what saints and theologians throughout the centuries have referred to as the *beatific vision*. It's the intuitive insight, apprehension, and experience of who God truly is. It's also the essence of what the Scriptures call "meditation."

However, the problem we face in our generation is that *meditation* has become a dirty word in many Christian circles due to its association with New Age philosophy. But in comparison to Eastern meditation which promotes the emptying of one's mind, biblical meditation invites us to fill our minds with thoughts of God and the Scriptures.

In contrast to Eastern meditation which advocates mental passivity, biblical meditation challenges us to deliberately reflect on those things about the Lord that will captivate our minds and emotions. This is nowhere better illustrated than in Philippians 4:8 where Paul wrote, "Finally, brothers, whatever is true, whatever is noble, whatever is right, whatever is pure, whatever is lovely, whatever is admirable—if anything is excellent or praiseworthy—think about such things."

"Unlike Eastern meditation, which advocates visualization in order to create one's own reality, Christian meditation calls for visualization of the reality already created by God."[51] It's allowing our imaginations to be touched by the Holy Spirit in such a way that we experience the reality of God revealed in Christ.

Meditation is a completely biblical concept, apart from which we will never fully experience the depths of communion with God that are available to us. We can't allow the distortion of a scriptural practice to rob us of the emotional and spiritual pleasure for which it was intended.

So, what is the nature of biblical meditation? In the Hebrew language, the word for "meditate" is *hagah*. It's found 25 times in the Old Testament, and it can also mean "to mutter or speak." The word conveys the idea of talking to one's self while deliberately *pondering* something. This was a practice that the ancient Israelites were encouraged to engage in. We see this first mentioned in Joshua 1:8: "'Do not let this Book of the Law depart from your mouth, *meditate* on it day and night, so that you may be careful to do everything written in it. Then you will be prosperous and successful'" (italics added).

Biblical meditation is really thinking and talking to ourselves about God. It's a conscious engagement of our minds with Him *mainly* through the Scriptures. The Bible was given to us to fuel our appetite for God. The more we reflect on what our minds have absorbed, the more we will encounter the Lord at a deep emotional level. We have truly meditated when we have slowly read, and prayerfully assimilated, what God has revealed about Himself in the Scriptures.

Donald Whitney, in his book, *Spiritual Disciplines for the Christian Life*, compares biblical meditation to the making of a cup of tea:

> You are the cup of hot water and the intake of Scripture is represented by the tea bag…. The more frequently the tea enters the water, the more effect it has. Meditation, however, is like immersing the bag completely and letting it steep until

51 Storms, Sam. *Pleasures Evermore* (Colorado Springs, CO: NavPress, 2000), 204.

all the rich tea flavor has been extracted and the hot water is thoroughly tinctured reddish brown.[52]

Biblical meditation can also be likened to a cow eating and digesting its food. A cow has four stomachs. It's in the first stomach chamber that large amounts of food are stored and softened. After the food is processed in the first stomach chamber, it's *regurgitated*. This substance is called "the cud" and it's chewed again by the cow. The chewed cud then goes directly into the other chambers of the stomach.

When we are truly meditating on the Scriptures, we are *regurgitating* those things that we have read. It's about chewing, processing, and reflecting on the things we've given our minds to, allowing the Holy Spirit time to awaken our hearts to the spiritual realities of what we've read. While many of us have been challenged from the pulpits to read our Bibles on a regular basis, very few of us have experienced the transforming power of meditation. As a result, we've often attempted to discipline ourselves to "glance" at a passage of Scripture or read a devotional book before our work begins in the morning or before we go to bed at night. But, if we'd be honest, much of our reading has been more out of a sense of duty rather than delighting in who God is. Maybe this is why we haven't even remembered much of what we've read.

What complicates matters even more is the fact that many of us have grown up believing any problem can be solved if we only acquire enough information. This is one of the primary reasons why the Christian community places such an emphasis on listening to sermons and attending conferences and seminars. We've come to believe that gaining information is the key to our spiritual growth and the answer to our personal problems.

While it can't be denied that information can, to some degree, help us grow and solve our personal problems, neither can it be denied that knowledge *alone* does not have the ability to make us more fully alive in God. Think about it. We have more information

---

52 Whitney, Donald S. *Spiritual Disciplines for the Christian Life* (Colorado Springs, CO: NavPress, 1991), 44.

available to us today than at any other time in human history. "Yet no one would dare to claim that we're generally more spiritually mature than Christians in the past."[53] The truth is—none of us will *truly* live until we have seen and experienced the superior beauty of God revealed in the Scriptures.

MEDITATING ON GOD THROUGH THE SCRIPTURES

Thinking about God is transforming! This was never more clearly illustrated than in the life of George Mueller, a godly man who established a number of orphanages in England in the 19th century. Mueller was someone who experienced the happiness and satisfaction of thinking about God. His adventure with encountering the pleasure of God's presence through meditating on the Scriptures began with a life-changing discovery in 1841:

> While I was staying in Nailsworth, it pleased the Lord to teach me a truth, irrespective of human instrumentality, as far as I know, the benefit of which I have not lost, though now... more than forty years have since passed away.
>
> The point is this: I saw more clearly than ever, the first great and primary business to which I ought to attend every day was, to have my soul happy in the Lord. The first thing to be concerned about was not, how much I might serve the Lord, how I might glorify the Lord; but how I might get my soul into a happy state, and how my inner man might be nourished. For I might seek to set the truth before the unconverted, I might seek to benefit believers, I might seek to relieve the distressed, I might in other ways seek to behave myself as it becomes a child of God in this world; and yet, not being happy in the Lord, and not being nourished and strengthened in the inner man day by day, all this might not be attended to in a right spirit.
>
> Before this time my practice had been, at least for ten years previously, as an habitual thing, to give myself to prayer, after having dressed in the morning. Now I saw, that the most important thing I had to do was to give myself to... medi-

---

53 Boyd, Gregory A. *Present Perfect* (Grand Rapids, MI: Zondervan, 2010), 98-99.

tation...that my heart might be brought into experimental, communion with the Lord. I began therefore, to meditate on the New Testament, from the beginning, early in the morning.

The first thing I did...was to begin...searching, as it were, into every verse, to get blessing out of it;...not for the sake of preaching on what I had meditated upon; but for the sake of obtaining food for my own soul. The result I have found to be invariably this, that after a very few minutes my soul has been led to confession, or to thanksgiving, or to intercession, or to supplication; so that though I did not, as it were, give myself to prayer, but to meditation, yet it turned almost immediately more or less into prayer.

As the outward man is not fit for work for any length of time, except we take food, and as this is one of the first things we do in the morning, so it should be with the inner man. We should take food for that, as every one must allow.... considering what we read, pondering over it, and applying it to our hearts....[54]

In light of what George Mueller discovered, I believe it's imperative that you try as much as possible to "participate in the experience" mentioned in the passage you're reading. For example, picture what it must have been like when the scales fell from the blind man's eyes and the flashes of shapes and colors bombarded his mind for the very first time. Try to feel the shame of the woman caught in adultery and then the sheer joy and relief she felt as Jesus loved her and liberated her from her sin (John 8:1-11). Imagine the smell of the fish and bread as they were multiplied by Christ and served to the multitudes (Matthew 14:13-21). Or, attempt to sense the surge of energy the leper felt throughout his body as his rotting skin suddenly became transformed into the skin of a baby. Let your senses experience the utter amazement and delight of this man as he was "tenderly touched" and pronounced clean by Jesus (Mark 1:40-42).

---

54 *Autobiography of George Mueller*, compiled by Fred Bergen (London: Jay Nisbet Co., 1906), 152-154.

It's also critical, as we mentioned in the previous chapter, that we always meditate on the Scriptures through the *lens* of Christ: "fixing our eyes on Jesus, the pioneer and perfecter of faith.... Consider him" (Hebrews 12:2-3).

> It is not Sacred Scripture which is God's original language and self-expression, but rather Jesus Christ. As one and Unique, and yet as one who is to be understood only in the context of the whole created cosmos, Jesus is the Word, the Image, the Expression and the Exegesis of God (See John 14:6; Colossians 1:15-20; Hebrews 1:13).[55]

As a follower of Christ, I have a high regard for Scripture. I've been committed to a study of both the Old and New Testaments for years. But everything we read has to be *filtered* through Jesus, the living Word of God in person. So when we approach the Old Testament, for example, we have to interpret everything through the following words of Christ: "You have heard that it was said to those of old, ... *But I say ...* " (Matthew 5:21-22; 27-28; 31-32; 33-34; 38-39; 43-44, italics added, NKJV).

"Jesus is what God has to say!"[56] This truth is powerfully illustrated for us in the story of the Transfiguration of Christ. Jesus took Peter, James, and John up a high mountain and He "...was transfigured before them. His clothes became dazzling white, whiter than anyone in the world could bleach them" (Mark 9:2-3).

> Perhaps the strangest aspect of the Transfiguration is the appearance of Moses and Elijah, who have a conversation with Jesus. The appearance of these two towering figures from the Old Testament contains some obvious and powerful symbolism. Moses the lawgiver and Elijah the prophet are representative figures signifying the Law and the Prophets, or what Christians commonly call the Old Testament....On Mount Tabor, Moses and Elijah are summoned from the Old

55 Dubay, Thomas. *The Evidential Power of Beauty* (San Francisco, CA: Ignatius Press, 1999), 300.
56 Zahnd, Brian. *Sinners in the Hands of a Loving God* (Colorado Springs, CO: WaterBrook, 2017), 59.

Testament to give their final witness to the anointed Christ who will fulfill what they had begun.

…But initially Peter misinterpreted what the presence of Moses and Elijah meant….Peter's first impulse was to build three memorial tabernacles on Tabor, treating Moses, Elijah, and Jesus as approximate equals….But Mark tells us how Peter's suggestion for a triumvirate of Moses, Elijah, and Jesus was rebuked on Mount Tabor: "And a cloud overshadowed them, and a voice came out of the cloud: 'This is my beloved Son; listen to him' And suddenly, looking around, they no longer saw anyone with them but Jesus only."

…Jesus is not a mere echo of Moses. Jesus is taking the revelation of God's nature and God's will beyond where the Torah ever could. Jesus is not giving the word of God through a Bronze Age cultural filter. Jesus is the Word of God made flesh! This is among the most radical and central claims that Christians make concerning Jesus Christ.

…Though Moses taught that adulterers, rebellious children, and other sinners should be stoned to death, God says to us, "Listen to Jesus!" And Jesus says, "I desire mercy, not sacrifice."

…Though Elijah called down fire from heaven to burn up his enemies, God says to us, "Listen to Jesus!" And what Jesus says is "Love your enemies." When a Samaritan village refused hospitality to Jesus and his disciples, James and John wanted to go "shock and awe" on the Samaritans and call down fire from heaven. They did so by finding biblical warrant from the actions of Elijah in the first chapter of 2 Kings. But Jesus didn't say, "Well, that's a biblical principle, all right. So let's Nuke 'em." No, Jesus, says something else: "You do not know what manner of spirit you are of. For the Son of Man did not come to destroy men's lives but to save them."[57]

"To say it as plainly as I know how, the Old Testament is not on par with Jesus. The Bible is not a flat text where every passage carries the same weight."[58] This is why Christ can challenge certain

---

57 Ibid., 51-57; Mark 9:2-3, 7-8; Matthew 9:13; Matthew 5:44.
58 Ibid., 55

Hebrew Scriptures and reinterpret others. And this is why *meditation* requires that we *wrestle* with the text.

MEDITATING ON GOD THROUGH CREATION

While meditation is primarily engaging God through the Scriptures, it can also take on other forms. Another way we can encounter God is by reflecting on His creation. And for me, this is when I truly feel alive in God.

I love the outdoors! I'd rather be out in the elements than stuck behind a desk. Almost every morning I find myself opening the door to our deck and breathing in the air of a fresh, new day. I love taking walks in the country, catching glimpses of deer and other intriguing wildlife. I love being serenaded by birds as they sing their sacred songs. I also enjoy walking along a nearby lake and taking in the sounds and smells of the waves splashing on the shore.

When I feel the tug on my heart to retreat into nature, I often wonder if I inherited this impulse from some of my ancestors or if it's a part of my spiritual DNA that calls me back to the *Garden*. But regardless of its origin, I love when nature beckons me to escape from the busyness of life to experience the splendor of God's creation.

Gregory Boyd, in his book, *Present Perfect*, also describes the impact of one particular experience with the wonder of nature:

> I used to run in ultramarathons (ranging from 50 to 100 miles)—don't ask me why. To train, I'd occasionally go on three-to six-hour runs through the woods.
>
> One fall morning, as I ran my laps on a beautiful five-mile trail that circled a lake, I prayed and enjoyed the scenery, though my mind was mostly focused on an upcoming race. I wondered whether I could win and what my strategy should be. I thought about what had and hadn't worked in previous races, and I worried that perhaps I hadn't trained enough. I wondered if the soreness in my left Achilles' tendon would improve or worsen—all the sort of things runners typically obsess about.

About two hours into my run, however, something unusual happened. I noticed a cricket chirping. For reasons that still escape me, I slowed down to pay closer attention.

Immediately I noticed another cricket, then another. In a moment I was surrounded by a choir of crickets! It seemed to me they had just started singing, though I knew this couldn't be true. They had to have been chirping throughout my run—but I just hadn't been listening. As I came to a halt, I giggled in amazement at how deaf I'd been.

Then something else remarkable occurred. As I stood in the middle of the trail, my ears opened up to an explosion of sounds—marvelous sounds. It seemed as though a million frogs were croaking their hearts out in the lake. They were so loud! How had I not noticed them before? A dozen or so bees hummed gently as they flittered in and out of a flowerbed in front of me. Distant grasshoppers contributed an odd, random buzzing. A magnificent, diverse choir of birds was proclaiming the wonders of creation. It was stunning. How had I missed all this until now?

My eyes also opened. I became aware of magical streaks of light from the new morning sun piercing the foliage overhead. A light mist hovered on the surface of the water. A swarm of gnats danced in the morning sun just off shore, and farther out on the lake, veiled in the mist, I spotted a family of geese. A nearby hummingbird darted in and out of radiant red and yellow flowers. A squirrel raced across an overhead branch. A couple of dragonflies danced with each other on a nearby plant. Gazing down, I noticed an ant carrying a leaf at least twenty times its size, and in that moment it seemed I'd never seen anything quite so amazing! I quickly became aware that this little fellow was just part of an entire civilization of insects that were scurrying about, busy with their various tasks on the edge of the trail. How had I been blind to all this living art before now?

My sense of smell came alive as well. I became acutely aware that I was breathing in a spectacular array of fragrances. Flowers, leaves, bark, morning dew, the lake—what a feast! I had smelled all these before, of course, but never like this!

The moment felt sacred. I felt I was waking up to God's presence permeating all things and reflected in all things. It seemed I was, for the first time, waking up to the way the world is supposed to be experienced—the way it really is. Overwhelmed by this sense of God's presence and breathtaking beauty, I began to weep.

I'm not sure how long the experience lasted, for I wasn't aware of the passage of time. But at some point the wonder began to fade, and my awareness of the world returned to "normal." For a little while I tried to recover the sense of wonder, like a person wanting to return to a dream they don't want to wake up from. But it was no use. Yet when I resumed running I did so with a new awareness that has profoundly affected my life ever since.

I realized that my trivial, self-centered mental chatter about the past and future—like a dark cloud blocking the sun—had kept me from seeing the glory of God that surrounded me every second of every day. Never before had I realized the extent to which our focus determines what we experience— and do not experience—in any given moment. Never before had I seen how being absorbed in the past or future causes us to miss the wonder of the present.[59]

Having just read about these life-changing encounters with God, are you ready to join with those who, over the years, have engaged God at a deep heart level? Are you ready to explore the vast possibilities that await you as you seek to practically experience God and the transforming power of His presence? Let me offer several suggestions that can help you.

Practical Helps

If you want to *behold God* in very tangible ways, it's essential to remind yourself that you are enveloped in your Father's love every moment of the day. He is closer to you than your very breath! Try

---

59 Taken from Present Perfect by Gregory Boyd Copyright © 2010 by Gregory A. Boyd. Used by permission of Zondervan. www.zondervan. com, pp. 11-14.

to be aware of His continual presence, but don't attempt to feel His presence. In fact, don't try to do anything. Simply acknowledge the fact that He lives in you and you are His delight!

Furthermore, as you approach the Scriptures for the purpose of meditating on the beauty of the Lord, you are going to have to do whatever is necessary to help calm your mind so you can concentrate and put yourself in a posture of reflection. As I mention in my book, *Enjoying God,*

> You're going to find that your mind will be thinking about all the activities of the upcoming day, or it will still be racing from all the events of the past few hours. Often a small to-do list will begin building in your mind. In order to remove this distraction, keep a piece of paper and a pen nearby. Record the things you need to do on the paper so that your heart and mind will be free to commune with your Father.
>
> One of the best things you can do is listen to good worship music. Some of you may prefer to play your guitar or the piano. Do whatever works for you. Music helps me focus on the Father…. The important thing is to find something that will help calm your heart and mind and assist you in transitioning from life's racetrack to God's resting place.[60]

If the place you have chosen to be with your heavenly Father subjects you to continual distractions, move it. If a specific time of day is inconvenient for you, then change it. If a particular posture is uncomfortable for you, alter it. Do whatever is necessary to make things conducive for encountering the Lord.

Another thing I would encourage you to do when reading the Scriptures is to personalize the passage. Whenever possible, replace personal pronouns with your own name. God never intended for the Scriptures to appear impersonal.

As you're meditating on a particular passage, absorb what you're reading and soak it in. Savor the words and turn them over in your mind. At some point, take what you're reflecting on and

---

60 Hill, S. J. *Enjoying God* (Lake Mary, FL: Passio, Charisma Media/ Charisma House Book Group), 168.

turn it into a *dialogue* with God. Remember, prayer is first and foremost conversation with the One who loves being with you.

The story is told of a Christian man who, for years, had struggled in prayer. One Sunday he went to his pastor after the morning service and asked if he could be given some practical help on how to pray. His pastor proceeded to go into his study and return with a thick theological book on prayer written by a Swiss theologian. The man took the book home, but after reading just three pages, he put it down and didn't read it again. He became frustrated because he had to look up thirteen words in the dictionary in the short time he had been reading the book.

One day this man was talking to a friend about his struggles in prayer, and his friend suggested that he go home, take an empty chair, place it in a favorite spot in his house, and then sit down opposite the chair and have a conversation with his heavenly Father.

Sometime later, this same man was stricken with cancer, and so he asked his daughter to call their pastor to come and pray for him. For some reason, the pastor was too busy, and he never came and visited the man in his home. One day, the man's daughter discovered that there was a traveling minister who lived nearby. She somehow got his phone number, called him, and asked him if he would come and pray for her father. The minister told her that he'd be more than willing to pray for him.

When the minister arrived at the man's house, he walked into his bedroom, noticed an empty chair by the bed, and assumed the man was expecting him. When the sick man saw his guest looking at the chair, he asked the minister to close the door to his bedroom. The man then proceeded to tell the minister the story of the empty chair. He also admitted that he had never shared the story with his daughter and even felt somewhat embarrassed sharing it with him. But he went on to say that for the last four years he had spent two hours a day sitting across from an empty chair, talking to his heavenly Father and had absolutely loved it! The minister was deeply touched by what he heard, and he thanked the sick man for sharing his story. He then spent a few minutes praying with the man before he returned home.

Several days later, the traveling minister got a call from the man's daughter. She told him that she had gone to the store to do some shopping and when she came home she had discovered her father had passed away. But then she admitted to the minister that there was something she didn't understand about her dad's death. She said, "When I walked into my father's bedroom, I found him on his knees with his arms around an empty chair."

When I first heard this story, I was reduced to tears. But I was also lovingly convicted about making things more complicated than they actually are. Father simply wants you to be yourself. You can share anything with Him. He likes that! Learn to be comfortable with being absolutely transparent and honest in your conversations with Him.

Let me also encourage you to use your imagination as you approach the Scriptures. While some of you may be uncomfortable doing this, there is nothing mysterious about it. God gave you an imagination as a function of your mind so you can experience more powerfully the reality He has created. Your reluctance to engage in this practice is more than likely due to the fact that it sounds like fantasy or something right out of "New Age" philosophy. Or, you just may be reluctant to try something with which you're not familiar.

Down through the centuries, the Church has tended to ignore the imagination altogether. This is due, in part, to the widespread influence that Plato and Greek philosophy had on Christianity. For example, Plato believed that God is beyond imagination. His thinking spilled over into a major segment of the Church, and this is one of the primary reasons why God appeared distant and separate from His "flesh and blood world."

Many theologians were profoundly influenced by Plato and Greek thought. John Calvin was one of those individuals. Calvin was a prominent theologian in the 16th century. He taught that God is beyond anything we can think or imagine. He believed that because God is transcendent, there is no way to represent God in our minds. His views still influence many to this day.

Greek thinking also placed abstract truth above experiential truth. It exalted the mind and looked down on the emotions. In fact, it sought to divorce abstract thinking from the emotions. But the Greeks were wrong! As a human being, you think with images, not abstract information. You're "wired" to be moved by experience, not just facts.

Science has proven that all of your emotions are associated with your thought processes. Every one of your thoughts has an emotional component to it. Your thoughts include all five senses. Your mind and heart are two aspects of the same thing. Your mind is the thinking part of your heart, and your heart is the feeling part of your mind. And, the more vivid an image is, the more power it will have in your life. This is why you need to take truth and reflect on it until it changes you.

Have you ever wondered why you can accumulate information from various sources and still not experience any permanent transformation? Have you ever raised questions about this to those you look up to? If you have, you've probably been encouraged to simply try harder. So you've attempted to discipline yourself to read more books and listen to more sermons; you've even tried to pray more. Nevertheless, you've ended up trying to relate to a God who feels distant and abstract.

But God wants to be real and "vivid" to you! Even though He's transcendent, He wants you to experience Him. This is why Jesus came. He was the perfect image and reflection of the Godhead. He was God "unveiled." He let men see Him, hear Him speak, and touch Him (1 John 1:1-4). And, He did all of this to let you know that His Father wants to be intimate with you.

Remember, Jesus said, "'Anyone who has seen me has seen the Father'" (John 14:9). So when you think of Jesus placing little children on His lap, hugging them, and talking gently to them, remind yourself that you're Father's child. Close your eyes and picture yourself approaching Jesus as He's sitting on a hillside. Imagine

Him holding out His arms to you and hugging you to Himself. Feel the embrace of the Father as He longs to awaken feelings of love in your heart.

Why is this so crucial for you to experience? It's because your view of God will determine your behavior. You will always be conformed to the "image" of who you think He is. The Apostle Paul reiterated this in 2 Corinthians 3:18: "But we all, with unveiled face, beholding as in a mirror the glory of the Lord, are being transformed into the same *image* from glory to glory, just as by the Spirit of the Lord" (NKJV, italics added).

What goes on in your mind and imagination shapes your life. So, let the Scriptures renew your thinking, and you'll not only see God for who He is, but you'll also be able to see yourself as He sees you. Psalm 139:13 makes it clear that Father *formed* your inward parts and *knit you together* in your mother's womb. You are His "masterpiece" in progress. And He loves the fact that you're His *favorite* child!

The Way You Love Me

Terri Churchill

Sometimes I think of you
Forming me from nothing
Shaping tendon and muscle and bone
To cover the vulnerable places in me.

I think of you absorbed in the details
Using your fingers to tenderly draw
The contours of my body.

I think of you bending over me
To breathe life into my lungs
The intimacy of your breath in my mouth.

This is how you have loved me
From the moment you dreamed a dream of me.

This is how you love me even now
As you swim in my veins
And whisper in my ear.
You are the secret I carry in my body.

BIO

S. J. Hill is a gifted Bible teacher with more than forty years of experience in the ministry. He has traveled throughout the United States and around the world, inviting people to enjoy God out of an understanding of His love and affections for them. He is the author of several books including *Enjoying God* and *A Love for the Ages*.

ALSO FROM ENERGION PUBLICATIONS

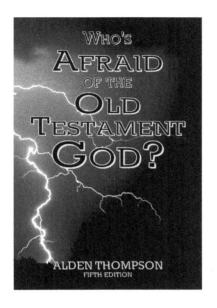

At the heart of even the Old Testament's darkest and most challenging texts, Thompson, like Martin Luther, finds there — "wrapped in swaddling clothes"—the living and grace-filled Christ.

Geoffrey Lentz, DMin
United Methodist Pastor
Florida

ALSO BY S. J. HILL

I loved this book. From the introduction there was a spirit of grace, of intimacy with God, that was ever wooing and drawing me closer to the Lord's heart. I felt, in a way, cleansed, not merely from sin but from serving God from duty rather than joy. This book goes beyond informing to liberating.

Francis Frangipane,
pastor and author

More from Energion Publications

Personal Study
Good Morning Lord!	Linda Estes	$12.99
The Jesus Paradigm	David Alan Black	$17.99
When People Speak for God	Henry Neufeld	$17.99
The Sacred Journey	Chris Surber	$11.99

Christian Living
Faith in the Public Square	Robert D. Cornwall	$16.99
Grief: Finding the Candle of Light	Jody Neufeld	$8.99
Crossing the Street	Robert LaRochelle	$16.99
Life in the Spirit	J. Hamilton Weston	$12.99

Bible Study
Learning and Living Scripture	Lentz/Neufeld	$12.99
Inspiration: Hard Questions, Honest Answers	Alden Thompson	$29.99
Colossians & Philemon	Allan R. Bevere	$12.99
Ephesians: A Participatory Study Guide	Robert D. Cornwall	$9.99

Theology
Christian Archy	David Alan Black	$9.99
The Politics of Witness	Allan R. Bevere	$9.99
Ultimate Allegiance	Robert D. Cornwall	$9.99
From Here to Eternity	Bruce Epperly	$5.99
The Journey to the Undiscovered Country	William Powell Tuck	$9.99
Eschatology: A Participatory Study Guide	Edward W. H. Vick	$9.99
The Adventist's Dilemma	Edward W. H. Vick	$14.99

Ministry
Clergy Table Talk	Kent Ira Groff	$9.99
Thrive	Ruth Fletcher	$14.99
Out of the Office: A Theology of Ministry	Bob Cornwall	$9.99

Generous Quantity Discounts Available
Dealer Inquiries Welcome
Energion Publications — P.O. Box 841
Gonzalez, FL 32560
Website: http://energionpubs.com
Phone: (850) 525-3916

CPSIA information can be obtained
at www.ICGtesting.com
Printed in the USA
BVHW032324010322
630318BV00008B/629

9 781631 994968